The Referral
of a Lifetime

The Referral
of a Lifetime

The Networking System That
Produces Bottom-Line Results...
Every Day!

Tim Templeton

WITH

Lynda Rutledge Stephenson

BK

BERRETT–KOEHLER PUBLISHERS, INC.
San Francisco

Berrett-Koehler Publishers, Inc.
235 Montgomery Street, Suite 650
San Francisco, CA 94104-2916
Tel: (415) 288-0260   Fax: (415) 362-2512   www.bkconnection.com

Ordering Information
Quantity sales. Special discounts are available on quantity purchases by corporations, associations, and others. For details, contact the "Special Sales Department" at the Berrett-Koehler address above.
Individual sales. Berrett-Koehler publications are available through most bookstores. They can also be ordered direct from Berrett-Koehler: Tel: (800) 929-2929; Fax: (802) 864-7626; www.bkconnection.com.
Orders for college textbook/course adoption use. Please contact Berrett-Koehler: Tel: (800) 929-2929; Fax: (802) 864-7626.
Orders by U.S. trade bookstores and wholesalers. Please contact Publishers Group West, 1700 Fourth Street, Berkeley, CA 94710. Tel: (510) 528-1444; Fax: (510) 528-3444.

Library of Congress Cataloging-in-Publication Data
Templeton, Timothy L.
    The referral of a lifetime : the networking system that produces
bottom-line results. . .every day!/by Tim Templeton.
       p. cm.
    Includes bibliographical references.
    ISBN 1-57675-240-2
    1. Relationship marketing. 2. Business referrals. 3. Business
networks. 4. Customer relations. I. Title.
HF5415.55.T45 2003
658.8'12—dc21   2003040434

FIRST EDITION
08 07 06 05 04 03   10 9 8 7 6 5 4 3 2 1

Copyediting and proofreading by PeopleSpeak.
Book design and composition by Beverly Butterfield, Girl of the West Productions.

CONTENTS

To the memory of Paul Wong,
the mentor who represented
"Mr. Highground" and made
a lasting, positive impression
in this author's life.

FOREWORD

KEN BLANCHARD

Coauthor of *The One Minute Manager®*, *Empowerment Takes More Than a Minute*, *Raving Fans®*, *Gung Ho!®*, *Whale Done!* and *Full Steam Ahead!*

I am thrilled that Tim Templeton's book *The Referral of a Lifetime* is the first in the Blanchard series with Berrett-Koehler. In starting this series, I was committed to help bring to leaders and managers short, easy-to-understand, parable-type books that offer simple truths and profound wisdom focused on uplifting the best in the human spirit within organizations. My hope was that all readers would want to share these books with the important people in their lives. *The Referral of a Lifetime* fits that vision perfectly.

With so many deadlines to meet, places to go, and things to do, we rarely have the time to stop and thank the people who have helped us achieve our goals along the way. *The Referral of a Lifetime* will help you realize how priceless those relationships are, both personally and professionally. While reading this book, you will not only learn to value relationships in a new light, but you will also find a number of truths that will help you simplify and increase your business.

Appropriately, I was referred to this wonderful little book by my good friend Vince Siciliano, whose relationship I trust and respect. It's my strong relationship with Vince that motivated me to pick up *The Referral of a Lifetime* and read it in one sitting.

Within the time it took me to read the book, I found myself reevaluating myself, our employees, and how we all view relationships at home and at work. I started to imagine the possibilities of my business and personal life excelling and staying grounded by simply applying the golden rule and always putting relationships first. I immediately wanted to share this book with my most important relationship—my wife, Margie—and then together we soon shared it with the rest of our family and the key leaders in our company.

The concept of putting relationships first is not a complicated one, but it's certainly one that's been taken for granted by many organizations. If you are interested in increasing client retention, building more referrals, and better serving your current client base, *The Referral of a Lifetime* may be the answer you seek. I guarantee it will help you stop and value the relationships you do have and help you not to let them slip away.

Thanks, Tim, for not only reminding us how valuable our relationships can be for one another but also for showing us how to make them valuable as they relate to achieving our business goals. I wish you success in your business and hope your valuable relationships last a lifetime.

CHAPTER 1

The Alternative to Cold Calling

It was another perfect morning at the California Coffee Café and Bistro, the favorite spot of the locals in the tiny, upscale California coastal town of Rancho Benicia. The fog was floating in from the harbor across the street as the regulars zipped in and out or stayed to chat, enjoying the ambiance of the little café.

Chuck Krebbs, the owner, was standing behind the antique oak bar that had been there when the town was a harbor for the nineteenth-century sailing ships and the place was a watering hole for the waterfront's sailors. Now, though, Chuck proudly labored between it and his wonderfully gilded espresso machine for this watering hole of a different era and all the friends it had made him.

He took a moment, glanced around, and smiled. Four of his favorite regulars were there right now.

In the center of the café with her large double mocha was Sheila Marie Deveroux, one of the most prominent realtors in town. Flamboyant to say the least, the eclectic woman with her raven black hair, her bright outfits, and her happy way of talking with her hands was hard to miss at her favorite table in the middle of the morning chaos. Chuck couldn't remember the last time he had seen her there alone. She always had someone with her, which of course Chuck liked since that meant yet another coffee drinker. But he couldn't help but notice that whoever the current person was, Sheila Marie would treat him or her like family. Just as she had always done with him.

"Chuck! A fill-up, please!" Chuck turned his head to another of his regulars—Paul Kingston, a casually dressed, thirty-something good guy, who was holding out his empty vanilla latte. Paul, a fixture each morning in the corner booth, with his sports page and his own special coffee mug, was one of those trustworthy men who knew everybody and seemed to know a little of everything, who loved spreading his knowledge around, and who had found a home in managing sales at the largest auto dealership in town. Chuck could not think of one bad thing he'd ever heard about Paul—except that he was talking about cutting down on his latte consumption. And that made Chuck laugh since Paul had just ordered another.

Out on the patio sat young Sara Simpson, Female Entrepreneur of the Year before she turned twenty-nine, holding court. It was Tuesday. Every Tuesday and Thursday, 8:30 A.M. sharp, that was where she and eight of her top salespeople met. A dynamo, all business and proud of it, Sara loved to have her early morning meetings with all her system sales consultants in the warm California coastal air under Chuck's umbrellas. "Double espressos all around, Chuck!" was always her "good morning." And he always made hers a triple, just to see if she noticed.

And then there was Philip Stackhouse, striding in on his expensive loafers for his large cappuccino-no-whip with a purposeful, time-to-get-the-day-started wave. Philip, who had just turned forty, had somehow turned his networking ability and his early years hustling securities on Wall Street into being the guy to trust in Rancho Benicia for financial planning. Everybody knew it; everybody trusted him and told their friends about him.

"The usual?" Chuck called as Philip came toward him, saving Philip a few seconds. Philip gave him his trademark thumbs-up and bellied up to the old oak bar, popping the correct change on the counter as he waited for Chuck to deliver his morning brew, which Chuck did in record time.

As he watched Philip pivot and head purposefully back out the door with a smiling salute to the coffee "colonel," Chuck gazed over the scene, hands on his hips, enjoying the sight. That's when he noticed Susie McCumber standing alone at the bar, staring at the circles she was making in her coffee with her spoon. It was her usual—hazelnut with steamed milk—Chuck remembered, and moved her way.

"Hey there."

Susie momentarily looked up. "Hi, Chuck."

"How are you doing?"

"Fine," she answered, unconvincingly, continuing to stare into her cup.

Chuck leaned closer. "Okay. Now, how are you really doing?"

Susie didn't even look up this time. "Oh, you don't really want to hear about it, Chuck. But thanks for asking." She began to rap her fingertips nervously on the counter.

Chuck pulled a biscotti from the big glass jar at his elbow, placed it on a paper doily, set the doily on a little plate, and slid the plate right to her fingertips, bringing them to full rest and prompting Susie's eyes to look up to meet his.

"Yes," Chuck said. "I do."

Susie could see that he did. She gave Chuck the smallest of smiles and said, "Well, okay. The thing is, I can't deny any longer that I've come to a crossroads."

"What kind of crossroads?"

"The business kind. I may have to admit to myself that I'm not really going to get what I've wanted. And I don't know what to do about it. I wanted my own business so desperately. I wanted to feel some purpose beyond a nine-to-five job, wanted to work for a dream of my own instead of someone else's. You know?"

"Oh, yes." Chuck sighed, looking around. "I know."

"I wanted to make a living, not just a paycheck that could disappear at somebody else's whim. So I got up all my courage and all my savings and . . . well, I risked. I tried. But," she paused, fingering the biscotti, "it's not working. And I may have to give up." She shook her head. "I mean, I have to be the absolute worst at cold calls. I can't do them. I cannot."

"So don't."

Surprised, Susie looked up at that.

"It's more than about making money, isn't it?" Chuck said.

"Yes. Or it was supposed to be. But maybe I'm not cut out to do anything but just put in my hours and get by."

Chuck leaned against the counter behind him, crossed his arms, and studied Susie.

Finally, Susie couldn't stand it anymore. "What? What's wrong?"

Chuck grinned. "Less than you think. Susie, you don't know how familiar this all sounds. Look. I'm going to give you a phone number. You can use it or not. But if you do, well, let's just say that when I used it and I met and listened to the man on the other end," he waved an arm around at the busy place, "the rest is coffee history." He grabbed a napkin and a pen and scribbled a number and slid it over to Susie.

"His name is David Michael Highground. A good friend of mine referred me to him years ago, and now I'm doing the same for you."

Susie looked apprehensive. She'd heard so many pitches, read so many books, and listened to so many big ideas for making it "out there." How could she get excited about another one? She didn't think she had the energy for another letdown.

"No, Highground's system isn't like anything you've ever heard."

That definitely surprised Susie. "Are you a mind reader, too?"

"No, I just know exactly what you're thinking. It's just another pitch, right?

"But have you ever heard a pitch that talked about relationships?" he asked. "Or about building a business doing the right things at the right times for all the right reasons? *Have you ever heard a pitch that suggests putting the relationship first—making your growth foundation the golden rule?*

"Trust me," Chuck laughed. "David Michael Highground does not now nor ever will have dollar signs on his forehead! Yet he's the most successful man I know. It's not about money. He has all the money he will ever need. It's about purpose and personal fulfillment. That's what floats his boat now." He nudged the napkin closer to her. "It's your call. Let me know what happens." And he moved down the bar to wait on a new customer.

Susie stared at the napkin, then at Chuck, then back at the napkin. Absently, she picked up the biscotti, dunked it a few times, and took a bite. Chuck got busy again and Susie's thoughts went bleak once more. She swallowed the last of her coffee, then picked up her belongings, turned to leave, and remembered the napkin.

To her surprise, she reached out and took it. And with a glance back at Chuck, she left.

Inside her car, Susie picked up her cell phone, then put it down, staring at the number scrawled on the coffee shop napkin. A rush of thoughts—not the least of which was the thought of her cell phone bill at the end of the month— made her hesitate. Maybe she needed to admit to herself that her dream didn't fit who she was. She just didn't have the right personality—or something.

But the things Chuck said.

Well, she sighed. She definitely needed help, that was for sure. And she had nothing to lose, that too was for sure. So she dialed the number and pushed the Send button.

"Yes?" The response was surprisingly warm.

"Hello," she said, trying to hide the nervousness. "Yes, hello . . . my name is Susan McCumber. Is David High-ground available?"

"This is he," the voice responded, still just as friendly.

She paused, enjoying the warmth. She wasn't used to that sound from a stranger. She had spoken with far too many strangers who hated receiving cold calls as much as she hated making them. She took a calming breath. "Mr. Highground, I hope this isn't a bother. You see, Chuck at the coffee shop gave me your name, said I should talk to you, that you have helped him and thought you might help me."

She could almost hear his smile over the phone. "Ah, yes, Chuck. He's a good man. Any friend of his is a friend of mine. How might I help you?"

Susie realized she no longer felt nervous.

And to her surprise, she found herself telling him everything:

"Well, you see, I went into business for myself six months ago. But now I seem to have lost my momentum and I'm beginning to think the problem is me. What I mean to say is that I started out so well and the company I'm affiliated with is fantastic and the people are so helpful . . . and I really believe in what we're doing. But I'm not making it work somehow. I've gotten off track and I can't seem to get back on. I feel like . . . like . . ." She made herself say the word she had been dodging for weeks: "a failure."

Susie couldn't believe she had just admitted this to a complete stranger. But the weeks she had spent attending local chamber of commerce networking meetings and following the cold-call procedures she had learned in training without results had become increasingly frustrating.

To be around so many successful people who treated her with respect and encouragement made her feel upbeat. But each week the vision of her actually attaining the same level of success as others in the business community seemed to decrease because of her absolute inability to obtain and keep new clients. In fact, the several contacts a day she had been forcing herself to make had dwindled lately to nothing more than thinking about making them. And her workday had begun to consist entirely of looking forward to the next business mixer to hopefully get an easy lead, maybe a new direct-mail concept or a new book or audiotape that would save her. Day by day, she could actually feel her confidence draining away.

"Susie." Highground's warm voice snapped her out of her funk.

"Oh, I'm sorry," she said, embarrassed. "Really, forgive me. I just can't get my mind to stop thinking about it all."

"Susie—may I call you that?"

"Sure," she replied. "All my friends do."

"Susie, you're definitely not a failure," Highground began. "You're simply in a place that all people pass through at some time in their career and in their life. You're on the mantel."

"The mantel?" she repeated. "You mean like the shelf-over-a-fireplace kind of mantel?"

Highground laughed. "That's the image. The mantel is a place to reflect. It's where the good stuff happens. It's the best place to be for me to help you because in order to get off the mantel and move forward permanently, you need a new plan. And you will move forward, I guarantee it. Does that make sense?"

"Absolutely," Susie responded.

"Okay, then," Highground continued, "before we meet I need you to know that my help is not for everyone. My philosophy or way of doing business doesn't suit everyone's style or need. So before I agree to meet with you, I need to ask you a few questions. Is that okay?"

"Well," Susie said, "I suppose so."

"All right. "First question: *Do you like yourself?*"

Susie almost laughed. *What a question! Did she like herself?*

She listened as Highground went on. *"In other words, do you want to become more of yourself and refine the gifts you have been given instead of trying to imitate someone else?"*

"I've never thought about it that way," Susie replied. "I can't say I'm 100 percent happy with my current situation, but as for myself, well, yes, I do like myself, basically."

"Very good," Highground said. "I didn't ask if you were happy with yourself. I help people become more of who they are, to become genuine. That's what others are attracted to."

Susie perked up. *What a wonderful idea.*

"So, question number two, Susie. Ready? *Do you believe in your product and company?* Are you proud to associate yourself with all aspects of your organization?" he asked. *"It can't be only about making money.*

"You see, I am going to show you how to build lifelong advocates of you and your company, so it's imperative you are absolutely sold on it yourself. That way, even in the event you were to move on, all the people you do business with will feel that you moved them to a better spot with the products or service of your current organization."

"There's no doubt about that," Susie replied emphatically. "That was why I started my own business in the first place."

"Excellent," said Highground. "Now, question number three. And this is probably the hardest one. *Are you willing to 'stay the course'? Everyone is different so the system applies differently to each. The one key thing, though, that everyone must have is what I call 'demonstrated consistency.'*

"You will see results immediately, but the real lasting effects, the kind on which you can build your business and life, happen only when you adapt this marketing system on a daily basis consistently for about four months. Then it continues to build and deepen each month thereafter. So the whole system turns on this: Will you stay committed to a course of action that won't include cold calling or making others uncomfortable but will take a daily commitment on your part?"

Susie felt a bit overwhelmed. But there was nothing that she was hearing that she did not instantly like. "Well, yes. I'm ready to try," was her determined response.

"Well, then, Susie, so am I," was his reply. "We'll meet this afternoon, around 3:00, at the coffee shop if that's convenient."

"Yes, I can be there."

"Good. See you then."

Before Susie could respond, Highground was speaking again: "Oh. One more thing."

"Yes?" she replied.

"You're going to do great."

Susie tapped her cell phone silent. What was she getting herself into? But she trusted Chuck, and this Mr. Highground seemed to be a good friend of Chuck's. She caught a glimpse of herself in the mirror. "And," she told herself, "you certainly have nothing to lose."

She'd be there.

CHAPTER 2

The Combination to Referral Success

At 3:00 P.M. sharp, Susie walked into Chuck's California Coffee Café and Bistro and was greeted by Chuck and his warm smile. He waved, held out a steaming cup of her usual, and nodded toward a table nearby. She took the cup and looked in the direction of the nod.

There was a little two-chair table with a handmade Reserved sign on it and a large, white coffee cup. Susie glanced left and then right, and seeing no one near, she strolled over to it. The white cup was full of what looked like strong, black coffee. She set her coffee cup across from it and then sat slowly down.

"Hello."

Susie jumped. At her elbow stood a silver-haired, trim, nicely dressed man.

"I didn't mean to startle you. I'm David Highground."

She got up. "Oh, no, really, that's fine. I just didn't see you . . . " she mumbled at this mysterious Mr. Highground.

She glanced back at Chuck, who gave her a thumbs-up and rushed busily away.

Highground's smile broadened and he waved at her chair. "Have a seat, Susie, and let's talk."

She sat and so did Highground. She took a sip of her coffee, suddenly more nervous and less trusting than she expected. Yet she kept thinking of Chuck and because she trusted him, she decided she would keep an open mind.

Highground must have noticed this because the next thing he said was, "You're feeling hesitant, aren't you? I understand. It's the most natural thing in the world. But the reason I'm here is because a good friend of ours referred me to you, right?"

"Right," she answered, a bit embarrassed for being so transparent.

"Well, then, *I have a responsibility to him to take care of you.* Know why? No matter how great my business concepts might be, the relationship I have with Chuck is much more precious than any service or program. So I'll honor my relationship with him by helping you."

Sensing this was more than just a way to make her feel at ease, she said, "What do you mean?"

"I mean, this very dynamic we are acting out is the key to everything you will learn in the next two days. Let's turn it around. You value Chuck's friendship, don't you?"

"Yes, I do."

"Then if he asked you to do something in your power to do, wouldn't you want to do it and do it well?"

"Well, yes. I wouldn't want to disappoint him."

"Why?"

"Well, because I value the relationship."

"That's it. That is the exact point. If you understand that *your relationships are more important than your products or services* and you always put them first, your existing clients and all the new people that come into your life will see this, realize you're the real thing by your actions, and enjoy referring their friends, associates, and acquaintances to you. When someone they know needs your products or services, they know you'll treat them right." He thought a moment. "Want an analogy?"

"Sure."

"Think of the world as a chicken coop. We can go searching for customers like they were chickens, running around trying to sell our products to every chicken we can corner. If we catch one, we can have a good chicken dinner that night, but then we have to go through the process of finding and catching another chicken. On the other hand, if we build a relationship with those chickens, take care of them, plump them up, continue to maintain the relationship with them and be referred to every chicken they know—we'll have omelets for life. No longer will we have to find a new chicken every day."

"Well, that's vivid," Susie said with a grin. "Even if I don't like omelets."

Highground laughed. "Of course. I do like omelets, but you get the point, I hope." He sat back in his chair. "It sounds amazingly simple, I know. Not what we usually hear in business, is it? Most programs are hit-and-run. Hit 'em with our pitch, run to find the next customer to pitch again. Think about it. Most major companies have powerful marketing programs planned months, even a year, in advance. But their sole focus is closing the sale. No thought is put into nurturing the relationship with the client after the sale, which ultimately leaves the door wide open for the competition to take the client *and* the client's referrals as well. And how much time is spent considering the type of person you happen to be and how that helps or hurts you in the program? None. Sound right?"

Susie thought about the seminars and lectures and meetings she'd attended. Everything was market, market, market and sell, sell, sell. The client was a faceless customer. And the question was always, How do you find the customers? The focus was never on how to build and maintain relationships with the clients. "Yes," she had to agree. "I'm afraid you're right."

"But what happens when you flip that idea?" Highground said, flipping his wrist in a half circle. "The client first, then the product or service! Let me put this another way: *I want to serve you well because of my relationship with Chuck.* Tell me the truth. Would you have come here if we did not have a mutual friend?"

"No," she admitted, taking a sip of coffee. "Probably not. No offense."

"So, you are here, entrusting your time to me because of your relationship with Chuck. And if Chuck didn't value both of us, would we be sitting here?"

"No, we wouldn't," she said. "Relationships. That is great, but how can that work in the long run? Surely it's too good to be true."

Highground smiled as if he'd heard that before. "What you are experiencing right now is the foundation you can build a business and a life on. And that goes for new clients and existing ones. Ready to begin?"

Susie nodded slightly, still a little standoffish.

"You'll see," he said. "Just wait." And then Highground pushed a small notebook across the table toward her. "This little notebook is your 'working ground' for the next two days. And afterward, it will be your plan of action, all you have learned and all you need to know."

Setting down her coffee, Susie accidentally jostled some onto the new notebook.

"Oh, no!" she gasped, wiping frantically with her napkin.

Highground joined in and in a second they were both laughing.

"I'm sorry," Susie said.

"Are you kidding? What better baptism for your new business life—Chuck's coffee!"

"Hey, keep it down over there!" a voice called from the front door. Highground looked back and waved. "Ah, there's one of the people you'll meet now! Sheila Marie! How are you doing?"

Sheila Marie waved her response, turning quickly back to the couple with her and steering them to her favorite table.

"Susie, in the next two days, you are going to meet four very different people who have been exactly where you are, and that woman is one of them."

Susie looked around. "Why, yes, I recognize her. She's as much a regular here as I am."

"And there's another." Highground pointed to Paul, who was standing at the counter, paying for his coffee to go.

Somewhat surprised, Susie said, "Why, yes. I know these people."

"Think about it. Is that so surprising? You know Chuck. They know Chuck. And so do Philip and Sara, who are the other two. I bet you'll recognize them, too. And of course, they know Chuck, too. We all know an amazing number of people who know an even more amazing number of people. Yet they were all exactly where you are right now not too long ago."

"They were all like me? I find that very hard to believe. They look so . . . successful."

Highground paused, then said in his teacher's voice, "Do you think you have to be like them to be successful?"

"Why do I get the feeling that's a trick question?"

"Remember the first question I asked you?"

"Yes, Do I like myself? It was a very interesting question."

Highground nodded. "I have learned a very basic but important truth over the years of teaching this system. You cannot and should not change anyone. You can modify some behavior habits and fill in a gap or two, but not for long.

"*We are all gifted in certain areas and we need to be more of ourselves, not less,*" he said, pausing for emphasis before he went on.

"Do you see Sheila Marie over there? Do you know what was holding her back? She is what I call a 'relational-relational' person, and she was killing herself trying to be a 'business-business' person because she thought that's what she had to be to make a living in her profession."

"Relational-relational? Business-business?" Susie echoed.

"Okay, let me back up," Highground said. "I believe we all see business and relationships through four 'windows.' Others see us and our style through the same windows. When we are not ourselves, when we try to be someone else, no matter how we try to disguise it, we feel uncomfortable. So our clients cannot help but feel uncomfortable, too."

Susie frowned. "Did you say four 'windows'? What are the other two?"

"Okay, let's go through all four. You know the person who is always ready with a hug? He or she is relational-relational. In the middle are the relational-business and business-relational people. At the other end is business-business, the type who seems only interested in the bottom line."

"What am I?"

That made Highground grin. "That's what you have to decide. In fact, over the next two days you will not only decide which you are, but you'll learn how to embrace it and apply it to your work."

"So, I get to be myself and I get to work with people who know someone I know?"

"Right."

"And the reason it works is because it's putting people first? Relationships are valued over the bottom line. And that, strangely enough, will allow the bottom line to take care of itself?"

"With a little more help from you, of course, which you'll soon learn about, too. But yes, you're getting the idea."

Susie opened her notebook. Inside were four sections, each one with a picture of a combination lock under the words "The Right Combination for Success." She thumbed through the pages, then looked up. "Don't take this wrong, Mr. Highground, but it seems too simple. Why doesn't everyone do it?"

"You know that old saying that the trees are in the way of seeing the forest? Most people are too busy dodging the falling trees in business every day to think about the simplicity and rewards of just treating people right and doing the right thing. But this works—because it's built around you. And while it seems simple on top, it's very deep below. Remember the third question I asked you?"

Susie quickly thought. "Let's see. 'Are you willing to stay the course?'"

"This is where the simplicity either works or it doesn't. I'm not selling magic, Susie. My system works because it's based on truths that, when applied, give back significant results. That last part is why I asked you if you were a 'stay the course' sort of person. And this is where I begin to introduce you to the people who have lived it and want to share it with you." Highground pointed to the notebook. "Read the first principle, why don't you?"

The cartoon picture of the combination lock had a pointer arrow, pointing to the first number. And under it were these words, which Susie read aloud: "**Principle 1: The 250 by 250 Rule. It's not only who you know that counts, it's who your clients know that is important.**"

She looked up at Highground.

Highground leaned forward. "Tomorrow morning, you'll meet Sheila Marie. And that's what she'll teach you. Read on."

Susie turned the page. There was the same picture of a combination lock, but the dial had moved to show number 2 at the top under the pointer arrow, as

if the tumblers had turned. She read the sentence below it. "**Principle 2: Build a database and ABC it.**"

"That will be Paul," said Highground. "We'll meet him for lunch and he'll explain that." Highground pointed at the notebook again. "Okay, now. Principle 3."

Susie turned the page. There was the same picture of the combination lock, but the dial had moved again to show number 3 at the top under the pointer arrow. She read, "**Principle 3: Just Let Me Know. Educate your clients about how you work and your value to them through regular, tangible actions performed without fail.**"

Susie looked a bit confused.

Highground noticed. "Don't worry. You'll understand it all very soon. Philip will be explaining that principle and he is a whiz at it. Okay, read the last principle. That'll be Sara, and she's also amazing."

Susie turned the page.

The lock's pointer arrow was now pointing to number 4, and the lock was open. For some reason, she found herself smiling at that. She read, "**Principle 4: Keep in touch, consistently, personally, and systematically.**"

Susie said, smiling again at the opened combination lock, "Well, I certainly get the metaphor."

Highground cocked his head toward her. "And after you meet my four 'principled' friends, you will find out it is much more than just a metaphor. Lots of things will open up for you—when you remember the combination, of course."

Susie shook her head slightly, somewhat overwhelmed, and closed the notebook. "Do I keep this then?"

"Sure do. Bring it tomorrow, along with your favorite pen or pencil, because you are going to be writing some very important notes under each principle as the hours go by."

With that, Highground got up. "Well, I bet you're tired and a little confused. But I hope you're also excited about tomorrow."

Susie stood up, too. "Yes," she said truthfully. "I am. Thank you."

Highground grinned from ear to ear. "Don't thank me yet. You're just starting on the journey. Be here at 8:00 A.M. to meet Sheila Marie. I'll meet you afterwards, okay?"

"You won't be here?" Susie suddenly felt a little over-whelmed again.

"Sheila Marie will take very good care of you. Trust me. She's relational-relational. You'll find out very quickly what that means. She's a fun person and she really is excited about meeting you and helping you tomorrow morning." He cocked his head. "Know why? Because it's her nature. It's who she is." With a wave, Highground was already moving toward the door. "You're going to have a great two days, Susie," he called back over his shoulder. And then he disappeared.

Or at least that's what it seemed like to Susie. She looked quickly around. The coffee shop was still the soothing, fun place it always was. But something felt different. Susie reached down and touched her notebook.

"Isn't he a great person?" a voice said from behind her. It was Chuck, rushing by with a load of coffee mugs in his hands. "So is Sheila Marie. See you in the morning."

How did Chuck know? With a slightly bemused shake of her head, Susie waved at Chuck, picked up the notebook, and walked outside. As she walked to her car, she glanced around as if she might see this mysterious Mr. Highground again.

Susie's eyebrows arched high at that surprising reflex. "I guess that's a good sign," she said to herself. She was looking forward to the next morning. She truly was.

CHAPTER 3

It's Who Your Clients Know

The next morning, at 8:00 A.M. sharp, Susie walked slowly into the coffee shop and looked around. Sheila Marie Deveroux, dressed in a flattering pale blue linen dress and a bright scarf, was at the same back table, this time, though, with a different couple—a rather dignified gray-haired man and woman, both in their seventies.

Hesitantly, Susie stopped at the oak bar.

"Good morning, Susie. The usual?" asked Chuck.

Susie smiled hello and nodded, looking back at Sheila Marie.

"Yep. That's her," Chuck said, to Susie's surprise.

"You know about my appointment?" she asked.

"Sure," Chuck answered, handing her coffee to her and ringing up her payment. "You'll like her. But then, she's relational-relational." Before Susie could comment, he was off to help another customer.

Susie watched Sheila Marie quietly for a moment and realized why she looked so familiar. She recognized her face from what seemed like half the For Sale signs around town. And suddenly Susie felt quite intimidated.

This isn't going to work, she said to herself and actually took a step back toward the door. But then she caught Sheila Marie's eye, and instantly she was bathed in the glow of a thousand-watt smile sent all the way across the café directly at her. Or at least she thought it was for her. Susie glanced behind her, then to her left and her right just to make sure. Then she turned her eyes slowly back toward Sheila Marie. And yes, the woman was smiling at her.

Sheila Marie waved at her, held up a finger to signal "Just a minute," then stood up to walk the couple toward the door. They passed so close to where Susie stood she could not help but overhear the end of their conversation.

From what Susie heard, the well-to-do couple wanted to move to the area and start over for personal reasons. And Sheila Marie was listening. Oh, she was listening. She seemed to listen very, very well, and from the look she was giving the couple, she seemed to be genuinely moved by what she was hearing. At one point, she even touched the older woman's arm comfortingly.

"So you think that house can be fitted for our daughter and her son's special needs?" the woman asked.

Sheila Marie's answer was revealing. She didn't keep talking about the real estate market or a quick sell. Instead, she said, "If it can't, we'll find another. But we'll know as soon as my contractor friend takes a look."

The couple glanced at each other, relieved.

And then Sheila Marie added, her voice quieter, "I know I've said this before, but I want you to really believe it. Moving to a new area and knowing no one is hard for anybody, much less when you have such a crisis going on. When my clients buy a house, I feel I also am responsible in part for their new lives, so please don't hesitate to see me as your neighborhood connection. And beyond that, if I can ever help, now or a year from now with any difficulties with your grandson, just let me know. My assistant and I do this for a living because, to be candid, we love to help."

The old man seemed very pleased. "What George said about you is true, Sheila Marie. Isn't that so, Maggie?"

The older woman sighed with what seemed to Susie like thorough relief.

Sheila Marie seemed to revel in their gratitude. "We'll meet after lunch, okay?" she told them as they said goodbye.

Before Susie could move, Sheila Marie had turned the buoyant feeling her way and was striding toward her. "Susie? You are Susie McCumber, right? David Highground has a talent for describing people."

"Yes, I'm Susie."

"Wonderful. Highground has told me all about you. He says you have great things in your future."

Susie couldn't help but feel a bit buoyed by those words, even though she had doubts about the matter. "Well," she said, a little embarrassed, "he keeps telling me that."

"Believe it. I've never known him to be wrong. Come on, let's take a ride. I need to look at another listing for that couple, just in case the news on the house they picked is not good."

Susie could barely put down her coffee cup before Sheila Marie had whisked her through the door to her waiting car—a white Mercedes with a personalized license plate frame that said "Sheila Marie."

Nestled comfortably in the tan leather upholstery of the beautiful car, Susie said what she was thinking. "You know, I admire how much in control you are of your life, Sheila Marie. You are so successful and comfortable."

"It wasn't always like this." Sheila Marie turned her eyes toward Susie as they rounded the corner. "When I was referred to David, I was not in control of anything. In fact, my nerves were so frayed and my self-esteem was so bad that I could hardly function. But David said, 'Sheila Marie, the problem is you are a relational-relational person trying to convince the world you are a business-business person.' All my effort wasn't working because I was putting on the wrong face. I was not putting on *my* face. You know?" Sheila Marie shined that bright smile Susie's way. Susie couldn't help but smile back.

"But what does 'relational-relational' really mean?"

"Well, that's a good question, and I think Highground will explain it to you in full detail this afternoon. But for me, it means that I'm the kind of person who loves people and values relationships so highly that I will always, naturally, put them before my business and financial needs. But that always made me think that I couldn't be a good business-woman. Trust me, I was never at risk of putting the 'program' ahead of the relationship with my clients. Business-relational people and especially business-business people are always at risk of seeming like they are driven purely by profit. Not me. The problem was I wasn't making a living, no matter how much I loved the people I worked with. Then I met David Michael Highground. With some simple coaching, he helped me start up a system that fits my personality, my life—and within less than four months, my business completely changed."

They turned at the stoplight and drove into the town's nicest section of homes. "Do you really think, though, the same system that works for you can work for me and my industry? What I mean to say is, you're a realtor with big commissions on each sale and all that. I'm not sure it can be the same for what I do."

They stopped at a stop sign, and Sheila Marie looked at Susie. "Let me answer that question with some questions you should answer for yourself, okay?"

"Okay."

"Do relationships count in your business? How much of your product would one client treated well buy in a lifetime? How would you feel about a marketing system that lets you be you, enthusiastic but not overly aggressive? Would you rather be known for your interest in the well-being of your customers than for the fees you can make from them? Would you rather wake up each morning confident that you have a system that works for you, using the most powerful and most economical marketing system known in business—word of mouth?"

Susie smiled. "I take it these questions are rhetorical."

Sheila Marie cocked her head at her passenger. "In a way. But in another way, not at all. And I've saved the best for last. This is the one that David Highground wants me to explain to you:

"Would you like a trained sales force of 250 people you don't have to pay telling the people they know how great you and your business are?"

Susie almost laughed. "Who wouldn't?"

"Exactly," she said, pulling up to the curb of the property she wanted to eyeball.

"In my business," she went on, "people kept referring to their 'sphere of influence,' advising me to 'work' mine. I thought I was—until I met Highground. 'Sheila Marie,' he said, 'you keep throwing words around like 'sphere of influence.' Do you know what those words really mean?' Of course, I wasn't about to offer an explanation, knowing I was about to learn something valuable. *He then, very succinctly, articulated that a 'sphere' was a domain in which one could exercise control, and 'influence' was the ability to effect change on something, or someone, with apparent ease.*

"He then asked me, 'Sheila Marie, are you exerting some form of friendly control over those you know to refer business to you with apparent ease?' My blank look answered no. I have since learned what it takes to build and maintain a true sphere of influence." She turned her head toward Susie. "Have you heard this before?"

Susie pulled her new notebook from her satchel. "Mr. Highground gave me this notebook. And that sounds rather like the first principle in it. Right?"

"Yes," said Sheila Marie. *"Principle 1: The 250 by 250 Rule. It's not only who you know that counts, it's who your clients know that is important.* Or as I like to put it, it's not only the people who you know that counts, it's also who your client knows. And for a person like me, well, it's like having 250 by 250 potential friends. Everyday I look forward to who I might meet." She laughed at herself. "Oh, sweetie, I do love that part of my work. In fact, I can't imagine a life without it now. It's hard to believe that just two years ago I wasted money on scheme after scheme to find new clients— everything from direct mail to advertising.

"I even had a telemarketer working for me," Sheila Marie went on. "Can you believe that! Here I was, a person who hates cold calling, trying to motivate someone to do what I hate doing and even hate having done to me! Talk about ironic! And my broker actually asked me if I would train other agents!" She shook her head. "It seems incredible now. And what's worse is I almost did it because my 'great' tele-

Principle 1: The 250 by 250 Rule. It's not only who you know that counts, it's who your clients know that is important.

marketing skills—which made me look like some sort of expert—had paid off so little that I needed the money!" Sheila Marie looked at Susie and Susie looked at Sheila Marie. And they instantly broke out laughing. It felt good.

"Oh, good grief," Sheila Marie said, wiping the laughing tears from her eyes. "It's crazy, isn't it?"

"Yes, it is," Susie said, running her hand over the soft leather interior. "I'm beginning to think maybe it's crazy like a fox, though."

"Now you're understanding. Do you know that in a national survey that asked people who had just purchased a home using a real estate agent if they would use the same agent again, almost 80 percent said they would? But in a separate survey, home buyers were asked if they did use the same agent and only about 10 percent responded yes!

"Here's another way to look at it. If I only take care of the people I know and gain their business each time they make a move—the 80 percent—then I'll do fifty transactions a year. Not bad, when you consider the average realtor in this country does less than fifteen a year . . . which is where I was before I started the program. I could easily have handled the sales of the people I know if I had simply made a proper effort to keep in touch and maintain those relationships. Susie, if you compound all the referrals I could have had that my competition received instead . . . "

She sighed. "Well, let's just say, now I pay close attention to my past clients and the 250 people I know in my database." She looked at Susie. "Any questions?"

"Yes. What if you don't know 250 people?"

"I'm glad you asked that question, Ms. McCumber," Sheila Marie said in her best marketing-seminar teacher voice. And then she belly-laughed again. "How many people do you think you know?"

"Well, I don't know. Maybe one hundred if I really work at counting."

"You'll be doing that soon. And you'll be very surprised to find out that you probably know quite a few more than that. I certainly was when I tried to answer that question. Highground told me I knew 250 people. He was pretty close, I have to admit. He then taught me the 250 by 250 Rule—that if I simply take care of the 250 people I know and become consistent with the rest of his simple system based on relationships, I could actually motivate them, through taking an interest in them, to refer me to the 250 people they know. Are you good at math?"

Susie did a quick mental calculation. "But Sheila Marie, that's impossible. That's over 62,500 potential clients!"

"Isn't that wonderful? That's the number I could think of as my client base because they should be thinking of me if they ever needed a real estate agent. Why? Because one of their friends is someone I've kept in contact with or done good business with. And if I have done a good job with the first 250, if I have proven to be trustworthy and professional, they will all enjoy referring me. That's just good basic human nature."

"Okay, but Sheila Marie, I really don't know 250 people."

"Oh, yes you do."

"Oh, no I don't."

Sheila Marie giggled. "Oh, yes, sweetie, you do. That's exactly what I said, and you know what? I did know close to 150 people. I may not have kept up with them the way I should have, but I knew 'em. Then Highground taught me how to add new relationships very quickly and easily to my list with the three 'magic questions'—which you'll find out about soon, I imagine. I didn't have to feel like I was being pushy with anyone. And when I got through learning and enacting Principle 4, they all heard from me—consistently and without fail. And then everything began to happen."

Susie shook her head. "You've really got it figured out."

"Now I do, perhaps. I certainly didn't before I met Highground."

"But, Sheila Marie, I still say it sounds too good, too simple. Why doesn't everybody rely on that good basic human nature you mentioned and live on referrals and relationships?"

Sheila Marie opened her car door. "Come on in with me and we'll keep talking."

As Sheila Marie herded Susie inside the empty house and began to put her expert eye to the place, she asked Susie, "I have a good analogy. Do you work out?"

"Yes."

"Do you find it simple? Easy to keep doing?"

Susie looked at Sheila Marie rather nonplussed. "Well, not exactly. If I didn't meet my friend for Jazzercise three times a week, I'm sure I wouldn't. But I keep up."

"You have a simple routine and you're confident it will keep you healthy and trim, right?"

"Right."

"Then if it's that simple, why do the majority of the people in this country have a problem with weight?"

"You're saying it's because they don't follow a routine system?"

"Or they start one and then, as they say, fall off the wagon."

"I knew there was a catch," Susie said with a sigh, leaning against a bedroom doorframe as Sheila Marie inspected here, there, and everywhere.

"But such a nice one," Sheila Marie added.

Having seen enough, Sheila Marie made shooing motions toward the front door, which tickled Susie. She liked this woman. It was hard not to.

"I have a big concern as well as a confession to make," Susie blurted out to her newfound friend. "How in the world can I start treating all my old contacts like my best friends when I haven't as much as sent a Christmas card to anyone in the last five years!"

Sheila Marie burst into laughter. "Excellent. Now we are getting to where the rubber meets the road. We all went through the same process getting the system up to speed. You said it right when you used the word 'confession.' That's what you will do—you will confess through a simple letter to all you know that you have not done a good job of keeping in touch, but starting now, you will. Easy as that. Phil will give you a copy of a similar letter I sent out to those in my 'sphere of influence' before I started to influence them."

"Whew! That's a relief," Susie said. "I've been carrying around that guilt since we started talking. My mother must have done an awesome job." Again, almost simultaneously, they looked at each other and howled with laughter.

Once outside, Sheila Marie put her hands on her hips and stopped to enjoy the warm sunshine for a second. "Beautiful day, isn't it?"

Susie glanced around. *Yes, it was.* She hadn't really noticed before.

By the time she looked back, Sheila Marie was already in high gear, moving toward the car. Susie had to hustle to catch up. As Sheila Marie unlocked the car, she smiled across the car's roof at Susie and said, "Sweetie, let me give you another quick tip on how to add new friends to your database. I did this with what we in the real estate business call a 'farm,' which is basically a particular neighborhood of people with which a real estate agent has no personal connection. So the agent tries to build 'brand awareness' by pumping a lot of dollars in direct mail throughout the neighborhood in the hopes of getting responses. Big money, not a great return.

"Well," she went on, "Highground challenged me to build a 'relational farm.' And it turned out to be a simple, different, and supereffective idea. He had me commit to a ten-week period of making fifty calls a week into the same neighborhood I farmed, saying the following: 'Hi, my name is Sheila Marie and I have been sending you information regarding real estate in the neighborhood for quite some time. Do have a second?' When I got permission, I asked the following easy, qualifying question: *'If any of your friends or relatives were interested in buying or selling real estate, do you have a good agent you would refer them to?'*

"If they answered yes," Sheila Marie went on, "I thanked them for their time, assured them the person that they mentioned would do a great job, then deleted them from my list, saving further marketing expense to that address, and moved on. If they said no, I asked if it would be okay if I continued to keep in touch. It's called permission marketing. I now had permission to communicate and build a personal relationship. In less than the projected ten weeks, I saved a bunch of money and became an 'overnight' success because of my personal communications. Susie, I developed a relational farm in no time and became the number one agent in listings and sales in the Cliffview subdivision.

"You could use the same strategy with any current potential client list you have. Just insert the proper words that relate to your business and increase the number of people you have permission to call! As the saying goes, if you don't know who you're going to call on Monday morning about your business, you're temporarily out of business until you do."

"Awesome!"

"Susie, did Highground ask you the three questions?"

"Let's see. Do I like myself? Do I believe in my product? And, Can I stay the course? Those three?"

"Those three. And the last one is the deal buster, but it's like your exercise program. You probably enjoy it now, don't you? You'd miss it if you didn't have it."

"That's right."

"Then you'll do fine. We all get busy. And we think we don't have time to stop and put into practice some foundational truths that we really want to live by. All it takes is understanding yourself and then understanding the lifetime value of a relationship above a commission check. Instead of wandering around with dollar signs in your eyes as I did—oh, I was a mess—you stride ahead with a willingness to help people get what they need. And that's so much more fun, not to mention fulfilling."

As they cruised back toward the coffee shop, Sheila Marie said, "So what do you think, Ms. Susie McCumber? Do you understand Principle 1 enough that I can send you on to Principle 2?"

"I think so."

Sheila Marie touched Susie's arm. "See here, sweetie. You just trust the simple system that Highground is going to show you today and tomorrow and then shift that thinking of yours just a little and I am here to tell you that it will change your life. It did for me. Let me have your card. I'm going to keep up with you, see how you're doing, okay?"

They pulled up to the coffee shop. Susie opened the door, got out, and then handed one of her business cards to Sheila Marie, who handed Susie one of her business cards in return. Then she said, just before she put the car into gear, "Keep that card now, and just let me know if there is anything else I can do for you, including house hunting. Remember! It's not only the people you know that count but who your clients know as well! Let's keep in touch!"

And with an affectionate wave, Sheila Marie drove away.

"Susie!"

Susie turned around to find David Highground coming her way, and there was a man with him, the man he had pointed out the day before in the café.

"So, Susie, how was your morning?" Highground asked.

"Great," was her honest answer. "Sheila Marie is quite an interesting woman."

Highground laughed. "That she is. Did she give you a good understanding of Principle 1?"

"The 250 by 250 Rule. 'It's not only who you know that counts but also who your clients know that is important.' Right?"

"That's it. I want you to meet Paul Kingston, Susie. Paul, this is the young lady I was telling you about—Susan McCumber. Her friends call her Susie."

Paul was a rather short, average-looking man with thinning sandy hair, pleasant enough, but not someone that you'd remember upon first meeting him. He was the kind of man who gets underestimated. And that's what Susie did.

"Hello," she said.

"It's a pleasure to meet you," Paul said, clasping Susie's outstretched hand with both of his. Susie found herself looking at him again.

"Paul wants us to have lunch with him. Can you do it?"

"Yes. Certainly," replied Susie.

"Okay, then. We've still got about thirty minutes before our reservation, so it's a good time for your first assignment. And Paul and I have some things to catch up on. Got that pen or pencil I suggested you bring today?"

She patted her satchel. "Yes, I do."

"And your notebook?"

"And my notebook."

Highground handed her a tape, tape player, and a headset. "I've made this just for you. Mostly it's my favorite classical music. Go sit over at the harbor, listen to the tape, do as it says, and we'll be back to get you by noon. We'll have lunch at the Capri restaurant right over there." He pointed a few blocks down the oceanfront. "Okay?"

As soon as she took the headset from his hand, Mr. Highground and Paul were gone. She roamed over to the bench that overlooked the cliffs, the sailboats, and the beautiful California coastline that she loved so much.

To her surprise, she realized how long it had been since she allowed herself to relax long enough to enjoy the view. Breathing in the salt air and listening to the gulls, she pulled out her notebook and her pencil and then put the tape in the player and the headset on her head. And this is what she heard to a soundtrack of Mozart music.

Susie, for the next few minutes, I want you to take the first step toward making this system work for you. In the space provided after Principle 1 in your Highground notebook, you'll note the numbers 1 to 250 on the next several pages.

As an exercise to make you see and believe how many relationships, old and new, you have, I want you to list all the people you know—through school years, church, family, and your daily interactions such as with the grocer and the dry cleaner. Acquaintances count when you see them all the time, such as the convenience store clerk or your mechanic. My educated guess is you'll be able to list one hundred people fairly confidently, and the rest you may have to be coached to recover from neglect or forgetfulness. I have included a memory-jogger list of typical contacts—relationships that will help you get started.

I also want you to take comfort in the fact that when you are focusing on others, attentive to what they do as opposed to putting your agenda first, you will easily add new names to your list on a weekly basis. You will do this by reversing your focus from your own needs to those of others. But you'll also do it by invoking the three magic questions. I know you're concerned about how to get to 250 names, and there are many ways. But one wonderful way to get there is to get to know people through the magic of these simple questions. The next time you meet anyone new and have had time to briefly introduce yourself, ask them the following questions:

1. What is it you do?

2. What do you like most about that?

3. If you could start over, knowing what you now know, what would your day look like?

And here's the bonus follow-up statement to use whenever you choose: "Tell me more."

I guarantee you will make more friends. You'll be found more interesting and have less pressure and stress in your life when it comes to meeting new people and prospects. Because you have a system behind you, you will never walk into another trade show, business mixer, or cocktail party and face the stress of being perceived as a "pushy salesperson."

After you have had a pleasant exchange with each new acquaintance, simply state, *"I've enjoyed meeting you. Why don't we keep in touch?"* Then exchange business cards, and the next day send a note to your new contact, who found you so interesting because your focus was on him or her as a person instead of a "sale," and start to communicate. It's called *permission marketing;* it's enjoyable and it gives you an opportunity to build a relationship. At the appropriate time, you will have a willing person to listen to what you do for a living—without ever making a cold call!

So, enjoy my music and get to work!

Susie stared at the notebook's pages and all those numbers for a frozen second, wondering why she had spent so much time cold-calling and getting rejected when she could have simply asked the "three magic questions" and received permission to communicate. Then she started racing to put down the story of her relational life: her sisters, her pastor, her friends at her old job, her teachers, her doctor and her dentist and her insurance salesman. She listed Chuck down at the coffee shop; Jane, the hairdresser; Amy, the shampoo girl; Joni, her favorite waitress at her usual lunch spot. She added all the vendors in her business, her current clients, her past clients, all those in her dance club. Every time she thought of one name, a new trail of old relationships came to mind. *They don't have to be my best friends, she reminded herself. Highground just said they must know my name.*

She was on a roll. *My goodness, she thought. Look at all these people I know.* And she began to write faster—she couldn't wait to see how many she could name before Highground returned.

CHAPTER 4

Categories
That Simplify

By the time she felt a tap on her shoulder, Susie had listed
over 150 people. She couldn't believe it. Highground must
have read her mind again.

"Told you so," he said.

She took off the headset and stood up. "Incredible."

"You'll have your 250 easy with a little more work," Highground assured her.

"Ready for lunch?" Paul asked.

"Famished."

As they walked toward the restaurant, Susie asked,
"What do you do, Paul?"

Paul glanced at Highground with a grin and answered,
"I'm in the business of being comfortable with who I am so
I can help others achieve what they want to get—and get
where they want to go. Our Mr. Highground here says that
I'm relational-business. I'm with a tremendous company that
produces a variety of quality products, and it's through this

company that I have made thousands of people smile the day they bought my product."

"Paul manages new car sales at the Rancho Benicia Auto Park," Highground added.

"I certainly do."

Susie was taken aback by the whole exchange. Suddenly, this man did not seem so short or average looking. The confidence of this man almost unnerved her. She could only wish for such confidence in her own sales talk, and she heard herself blurt out, "Where does your confidence come from? It's infectious."

Paul laughed, affectionately clamping a hand on Highground's shoulder. "When I was at my own crossroads—or as Highground likes to say, 'on the mantel,'—this man came to me through a friend and spent time helping me as no one else ever had. He was the first to tell me that I didn't have to imitate anyone else, that the gifts I had been given at birth were more than enough for those around me if only I would trust and exercise them and be consistent in doing so.

"I spent a couple of days, just like you are doing, with Highground's concepts," he went on, "and it opened my eyes to a better and more simple way of doing things. I learned firsthand how not to put my products and my personal needs before my relationships with others because when I did, people could see right through me. They saw dollar signs across my forehead and automatically pushed away. And," he added, "I learned how to stand in front of clients or a group of salespeople and enjoy being me, a short, plain-looking relational-business type of guy who is extremely successful at managing and selling—"

"Yes," Highground added with a grin, "you certainly are."

"And proud of it. This all happened for me, Susie, when I followed our Mr. Highground's little system and trusted it to produce all the results I need. I am 'doing business from the high ground,'" Paul added, with a nod toward David Highground as they walked. "That's a little phrase a few of us coined in honor of your work with us, David. The high ground is where we all want to be strategically in business, but more importantly, it's synonymous with the 'high road.' You know, always trying to do the right thing."

Highground smiled. "Thank you, Paul. I appreciate that."

They had arrived at the restaurant door, and Paul gallantly held it open for them.

When they were finally seated, with a view of the harbor and the bluff, they could see on the horizon a freighter steaming out to sea.

Susie watched a few seconds, then she looked across at the mysterious David Highground and finally asked what she'd been wanting to ask all day. "Mr. Highground, I asked Sheila Marie about being 'relational-relational' and she said you would explain it all in detail. Would you? I'd like to know what I am."

Nodding, Highground turned his gaze to the freighter for a moment, then said, "I've been helping folks for as long as I can remember, Susie, and I finally concluded that it is futile to try to change people into something they are not. Since God provided all of us with our unique individual gifts, *what I should do is meet people where they are and help them be more of what they are.* Someone said that we are all three types of individuals—first, the one we are; second, the one others see; and third, the one we want to be. By taking the time to look at ourselves and asking others whom we trust, we can identify who we really are and how others see us.

And by doing that, along with being willing to change our habits, we can actually get very close to who we want to be."

Paul looked up momentarily from his menu. "And we can stop wondering what 'personality du jour' we need to put on to 'make it.' Hmmm. Look at the soup du jour—Boston clam chowder. I think I'll have that."

"Susie," Highground went on, "do you remember all four windows of business personalities I rushed through with you yesterday?"

"Yes and no."

Highground grabbed four paper napkins, pulled a pen from his pocket, and began to scribble. The first words were "relational-relational."

"The four types are split into two words," he explained, pushing the napkin toward Susie. "The first word represents how people see you and who you are naturally. The second word is your natural tendency in business relationships. The relational-relational person is one others see as someone who only thinks of relationships with others—how to help and how to be liked or even loved. These people rarely think of the business ramifications of their actions, or if they do, they will justify them immediately in some 'relational' way. So the second word has to be 'relational,' too."

He then scribbled "relational-business."

He pushed that napkin toward Susie, too. "The second type is a person who is very relational when meeting people and is truly interested in the relationship first but who, when the talk turns to business, will begin to think strategically."

On the third napkin, he wrote "business-relational."

"Note which comes first here." He placed the napkin on top of the other two in front of Susie. "The third one is the reverse of the second. It's a person who doesn't come off at first glance as interested in a relationship as much as in pure business but who will develop deep relationships after the business is established."

He took the last napkin and wrote across it "business-business."

"And the final trait is business-business, which is simply the opposite of relational-relational. These people usually have a hard time with our little system based on relationships until they justify the time spent with those they've affected in some sort of purely business way—which they always do." He placed this final napkin on top of the rest.

"So, is one better than the other?" Susie asked rather earnestly.

"Absolutely not. There is no right, no wrong. There is simply who we are and why we need to be comfortable with ourselves. But," he went on, "it's important to note that without consistency and a plan, all traits are equally ineffective."

"Note that," Paul suggested.

"And," Highground continued, "if you also identify the personality trait of the person you are working with, you will become comfortable and learn how to respond appropriately. We all have the ability to change our behavior patterns. When Paul meets a business-business type, he does not spend a lot of time warming up to that person like he would a relational-relational. He answers directly, isolates the issues directly, and asks for the sale directly. He is more at ease—and his numbers speak for themselves."

Paul looked directly at Susie and smiled widely, as Highground took out another napkin, wrote "isolate issues, ask/answer questions directly with one's personality in mind" across it, and placed it on top of all the rest.

"My biggest hurdle," Paul explained, "was that I was a relational guy. I met lots of people and I did not always invest my time with the right people—until I took the 'high ground' and started using this system to build a database, ABC it, and strategically lay out a plan the right way first, so I wouldn't have to do it ever again."

"ABC it?"

"That's right. And that's next. Now, let's eat!" Paul demanded.

The three finished lunch and ordered coffee. "The main thing I want you to know before we start," Paul explained to Susie, "is that because you were referred to me by Highground, I am at your disposal."

"And with that, I'm going to leave you two to chat," Highground said, getting up. "I'll be back."

"When?" Susie asked, wishing he wouldn't keep disappearing.

"Oh, I'll know when to come back," he said, as mysterious as always. And he was gone.

"A great guy, eh?" Paul said. "Well, he asked me to explain Principle 2, and so I shall. I'm going to show you how to do business only with the people you want to and on your terms! Sound good?"

Susie smiled. This man was warm, but he was also very businesslike when it came to specifics. She liked that. "So, you're relational-business. I wonder if that's what I am," Susie said.

The coffee came and Paul took a sip. "Well, for me, the funny thing about being relational-business is although I have 'business' tacked on to my trait, I did not always execute in a businesslike manner. It's not that I didn't know how; I just didn't have a system in place."

"But you seem very businesslike to me."

Paul gave her a nod. "Well, thank you. But I had to work at keeping focused, let me tell you. Basically, it's not easy to call up a client you leased a car to two years ago and expect to start up where you left off at the close of the sale. In the auto business, salesmen become like your new best friend during the sale, but it's hard to keep up that relationship afterwards. That's why only a select few in this business are able to acquire a high referral base of business. Unless you have a system and philosophy that work even when you don't want to, it just won't happen." Paul smiled, "Ready to hear all about Principle 2?"

"Let's see." Susie flipped through the notebook. "Here it is. 'Build a database and ABC it.' You're going to tell me what it means?"

"Sure am. What I'm going to show you is how to rate and communicate with your entire database and what happens when you do! Got your notebook? Turn to your 250 by 250 list."

She obeyed and pushed it toward him.

Paul looked it over. "Looks good. Now, Sheila Marie helped you understand the power of your database—that's what this list is, a database. What I want to share with you is how to make it work properly. You have to ABC it just as Highground taught me to do."

Principle 2: Build a database and ABC it.

"ABC it," Susie echoed.

"That's right, ABC it. Highground also convinced me that I needed a full-time assistant to help me follow up. That was a very big commitment, starting out. But when you get to Principle 4, you'll see how that might sound feasible to you, too. Even if it sounds crazy right now."

Susie frowned.

"Okay, let me see if I can put it into an image." Paul thought a minute. "Do you have certain people that are absolutely your cheerleaders, ones that would stand up and speak a good word about you, ones that feel so strongly about you and your products that they would refer you right now? These are the ones that have referred you in the past."

Susie perked up. "Sure, I'm thinking of several right now, several who already have, multiple times."

"Fantastic," Paul exclaimed, beaming. "Those are your As, your power base. *Your As are the ones that are most likely to refer you*. They are your advocates, your champions. You will find that, on average, your *A*s will account for about 10 to 12 percent of the people you know. They are the easiest to identify as they will jump off your list and say hello to you like an old friend.

"Now, who are your *B*s?"

"That's my line," Susie said.

"Oh, right. Excuse me." Paul laughed.

"Okay, well, *your Bs are individuals that you think can champion your cause as well as refer you if you educate them about how you work*. The idea is to learn more about them, be proactive in building a better relationship. If you keep in good, consistent contact with them, many will become *A*s. Your whole focus with *B*s is to move them to *A*s. This group is a bit more difficult to identify. You will find that your *B*s will account for about 17 to 20 percent of those you know."

"And the *C*s?"

"*In the C category are people you are not sure about but still want to keep communicating with*. Perhaps you have just met them or have been briefly introduced, but because you exchanged business cards you have been given the right to communicate. You are not even sure whether they'll champion your cause or refer you, even after proper communication and education, but you hope that they will.

"The last category is almost as important as the first. This is the one that actually gives you the ability to control your business to some extent. That is the D category. *The D category is synonymous with 'delete' or 'defer.'* These are individuals you are certain that you do not want to work with."

"You're kidding. I get to choose?"

Paul smiled wryly. "There's an old saying that we are judged not only by the people that we do business with but also by the people we choose not to do business with. So, yes. It's a no-thank-you list. An I'd-rather-not-do-business-with-you list."

"Wow."

"Nice thought, isn't it? To be able to say no?"

"Nice? It sounds impossible," Susie marveled. "But how do you set this all up? What do you say? How often do you say it, and what do they say in response?"

"Slow down," Paul laughed again. "We'll get to all those good questions in due time. This is a step-by-step process. Besides, Highground has already figured out all of that and made it easy to implement."

"Really?"

"Really. It's why we are sitting here. He's saving the best until last." Paul opened his briefcase. "Now, I've got something to show you. I brought along a printed copy of my database separated into As, Bs, and Cs." He pulled a stapled computer printout from his briefcase and handed it to Susie.

Susie studied it a moment and said, "Wow, Paul. You certainly have fewer As than I would have expected."

"That's by choice, Susie. The most precious commodity we all have is time. I communicate in writing and, in many cases, personally each month with my As. I am very careful who becomes one of my As. They must have demonstrated the ability to champion my cause as well as refer me and be a power advocate for me. These are the people I spend most of my time and marketing dollars on. I believe Highground has you set up to visit Sara Simpson tomorrow. She will show you what I mean."

"Okay," Susie said, "but what type of database do you use? What should I use? I've heard all this hype on CRM software—I think that stands for 'customer relationship management,' right? Should I incorporate e-mail?"

Paul held up his hand and smiled, "Whoa, kiddo. Like I said, all in due time. I do want you to know that there are a number of great programs available: Act, Goldmine, Outlook, Sales Logix, MyRMS.com, ACCPAC, eAssist, People-Soft, Sieble Systems, Salesforce.com, and more. Use the one that is most comfortable for you. The main thing is to pick one and use it. The only prerequisite is you must have the ability to set up fields that are titled *A, B, C,* and *D!* "

Paul set down his briefcase. "Before I had this system, I was letting business happen to me instead of doing business in a proactive way. Now I actually train all the new people at the auto park in this system. I get a real kick out of helping people get over the biggest hurdle in business—finding new qualified individuals to do business with regularly. And I'm not talking about 'spray-and-pray marketing' anymore."

Susie shook her head. "Thank goodness. I detest that."

"Me, too. What I'm referring to is having the opportunity to meet people on the strong recommendation of their friends and associates—and to do so regularly. Just like you were referred here to me by Highground. He spoke highly of me, didn't he?"

"Sure did," Susie confirmed.

"By the time I walked up to meet you, I was already delivered to you on a pedestal, wasn't I?" Paul asked.

"Well, yes. He couldn't say enough nice things."

"And that's a nice pedestal to be on, even if I have to make very sure to do my work in an excellent way so I don't tumble off it. That's what the system is all about. When we really think about our past, haven't all the significant relationships—business or personal—for the most part come from a referral? A middle person building you up without you having to do that yourself?"

"Absolutely," she again confirmed. *"It's not what you say about yourself that people believe anyway, it's what others say about you that they believe."*

That made Paul laugh. "My goodness, Susie, you sound like Highground! You're getting it! So doesn't it make sense to have a system in place that will allow you to do that every day? That is what ABC-ing your database will do for you. It will give you the ability to be proactive with all the people you know now and all that you will meet in the future. Now you will look at each of your friends and business acquaintances as a lifelong relationship. You will no longer feel rushed to push your business at everyone you meet other than the ones it makes sense to."

"Did Paul teach you your ABCs?"

It was Highground. He was back, standing by their table.

Highground looked at Paul and said, "Remember I mentioned that I might ask you to share with Susie, if you had time, how we helped you increase the size of your database by 'adopting' a list of your dealership's past clients? Can you do that?"

"No problem, HG," Paul fired back. He turned to Susie. "I was light on names in my list, Susie, so our Mr. Highground here had me ask the owners for a list of past clients. I developed a letter that the owner sent out to past clients that basically said how much he appreciated their business and how he just wanted to follow up to see if they had any questions or needs he might address. Then I had the owner, in the letter, 'introduce' me as the manager and the key contact if they had any questions. After a few days, I followed up by calling them all to answer any questions they might have and also to ask whether it would be okay if I kept in touch personally with them. Worked like a charm. I 'adopted' over seventy-five new people into my personal database and started to communicate immediately. I have leased or sold a new car multiple times almost everyone on the list and have received countless referrals. I brought a copy of the letter, written to a couple named the Tureks, for you to take with you."

Paul handed the letter to Susie.

"That's incredible, Paul," Susie said after she scanned the letter. "I could easily apply the same process with my clients."

Paul looked at his watch. "It's three o'clock, already? Where has the time gone? Susie, I have a little sales meeting in fifteen minutes. We thought you might enjoy being there. I'm training some new people that have joined our company—giving them an overview of the system. Want to join me?"

"Sounds great."

"We thought you'd say that," Highground said. "Shall we go?" For the next hour, Susie sat next to Highground, mesmerized by the confident Paul as he talked to seven new salespeople about his products, about their opportunity, and about the lifelong value of relationships instead of commissions.

Now Susie was getting excited. She could taste it. That would be her in front of those seven as soon as she could get the system operational.

After the session, Susie asked for Paul's card and put a big A on the back so he could see it. Then she smiled, shook his hand, and thanked him for a very revealing afternoon.

— FROM THE DESK OF P. J. STODDART —

Ken and Sue Turek
1007 Pacific Coast Way
Rancho Benicia, CA 92117

Dear Ken and Sue:

I want you to know how much I appreciate the fact that you chose our dealership to purchase your new BMW from. I, along with the members of our team, want you to know that if you have any questions, any problems, please feel free to call us directly.

It is to that end that I asked our new manager, Paul Kingston, to work with you personally in the event you have any questions or needs. Paul is a proven professional and we are proud to be associated with him. He always puts the relationship first with everyone he serves.

Paul will be contacting you in the near future simply to personally introduce himself and answer any questions you might have.

Thanks again!

Warm regards,

P. J. Stoddart
President
Rancho Benicia AutoGroup, Inc.

Highground and Susie walked down the street towards the coffee shop where her adventure had begun.

Susie had a million questions. "Paul said you had everything planned out—when to do what, how to do what, and all that. Is that true?"

"Well, yes it is." Highground smiled. He always enjoyed watching the light go on with his protégés. Susie looked and acted completely different from the way she did the morning before. She was starting to get the vision.

"All large companies have a marketing plan for at least a year in advance. They brand themselves with a certain image, and all employees have to align themselves with it, yet they are expected to figure out all by themselves how to find their customers. What I do for folks like you is give you a powerful marketing plan with a personalized brand based on one truth—the golden rule—that allows you to not have to think about it after you initiate it. And if even that is too overwhelming at first or if you just don't want to do it yourself, you can get outside help to implement it. But that's jumping ahead to Principle 4."

Susie pulled her notebook from her satchel, flipped to the right page, and read. "Let's see. Principle 4: Keep in touch, consistently, personally, and systematically."

Highground grinned from ear to ear. "That's right. But before we can get there, we have to learn what to say when we do try to stay in touch, don't we? That's the next principle."

Susie flipped back a few pages and read to herself, "*Principle 3: Just Let Me Know. Educate your clients about how you work and your value to them through regular, tangible actions performed without fail.*" She looked up at Highground and sighed.

Highground cocked his head toward her, understanding everything she was feeling. "Susie, what I would like you to do is go to a quiet place tonight and think about the day. I have given you a little outline for some goals. You'll find it in your notebook. Continue the exercise tonight and journal your plans. And I'll see you at 8:00 sharp tomorrow morning. Philip and Sara will be teaching you the next two very important principles. And don't worry. They do a super job."

"I want you to know how much I appreciate your help," Susie said.

"The pleasure is all mine," Highground said with a smile. "I believe you have experienced several 'lightbulb' moments today. See you in the morning."

Susie started to walk away and turned to mention one more thing, but Highground was gone—again. She smiled and shook her head. *Who is this guy anyway? What a day,* she thought, *what a day!*

At home that night, she sat down, opened her notebook, and found her assignment in a section marked "Goals." Attached was a little note from Highground:

— ᏮᎷᎷᎶ —

Dear Susie,

By now, you have found out that you know a lot more people than you thought you knew, and you've begun to grasp the power of the 250 by 250 Rule of Principle 1. You also know that having a list is not enough. You know Principle 2, that the list has to be ABC-ed to make it work for you. You know now how much nicer and easier it is to be pulled in by your clients instead of pushing your way in.

Before we go on, here's your assignment. I'm a big believer in the power of goals to make things happen. One of my favorite sayings is "If you don't know where you are going, any road will take you there." And another great favorite of mine is "Success is a goal with a deadline."

So we are going to create some goals, short ones. Long-range goals are great for seeing the big picture, but short-range ones get things going.

On the next two pages are two sheets designed to get you going. Changing your perspective is helped by imagining yourself already putting these principles into action in your life.

Postdate Goal 1 for two weeks from today. Postdate Goal 2 for eight weeks from today. And then put on your best imagining cap and project yourself and where you'd like to be on both those dates. Don't be bashful. You have what it takes.

Good luck!

Best,

D. M. Highground

Susie turned the page, found a form with blanks all set up, and began to write. This is what her two goals pages looked like after she was finished:

GOAL 1

Goal: *Finish my 250 by 250 list and then organize the names. Begin to put my new mind-set into action.*

Goal Date: *two weeks from today.*

The date is *July 1* **and I have:** *spent the last 2 weeks laying out my goal and spending much-needed time laying out my new marketing plan for my business. I now have fully realized the importance of a relationship over my short-term financial gain, and I know that it is good business to spend more time developing relationships for their life-*

time value. I have taken to heart that I truly can communicate with thousands of people on a personal level through the 250 on my list.

I have already experienced: *a complete reversal of the boxed-in mindset I had at the coffee shop two weeks ago. I look forward to my day.*

I feel: *that I have a handle on where I am going because I now have a proven plan on how I operate each day.*

I am excited about: *having this system fully operational on a daily basis and seeing regular results from it.*

My associates and colleagues are: *impressed with my new direction. They are asking questions about my new approach. They are seeing a confidence in me that is attributable to being myself rather than trying to imitate others.*

I am determined to: *each day make progress in reaching the other goals I have taken the time to write out and review regularly.*

GOAL 2

Goal: *Have my 250 by 250 database ABC-ed and in use.*

Goal Date: *eight weeks from today.*

The date is *August 15* **and I have:** *just reviewed my database of over 250 names. I have all four categories listed—A, B, C, and the Ds—and can access them by category with the push of a button. I can mail merge a letter in seconds. I now know through experiential knowledge that this is the only marketing plan I will ever need. I have already started to communicate with the people on my list through an initial mailing outlining their importance to me.*

I have already experienced: *fifteen solid referrals in the process of setting up and communicating with my database of 250 people. Calling* these referrals has been so enjoyable because I have been asked to do so. As Highground said, I have been pulled in instead of pushing in.

I feel: *more in control of my day and more positive because I actually have a proven proactive daily plan for my business and have experienced results. I feel good about myself, as if I have found a place I fit in the business world by being myself.*

I am excited about: *learning and implementing a systematic program that keeps me in touch regularly, with everyone I know that will make all that I learned into a true system for my life. I no longer have to apologize for not following up because my system does so for me. Everyone congratulates me on keeping in touch with them.*

My associates and colleagues are: *viewing me as a competent businessperson because of the discipline I have developed in my business. Several have asked me to share my secret.*

I am determined to: *stay the course and become extremely competent in this process and further develop my style and personal skills around it.*

Susie set down her pencil and smiled. The assignment actually worked. She had imagined herself in the future. And she liked what she had imagined. She put down the notebook, turned out the light, and fell asleep looking forward—for the first time in a long time—to the day ahead.

CHAPTER 5

Creating
Power Advocates

Susie awoke earlier than usual the next morning. The sun had not quite risen over the mountains to the east of Rancho Benicia.

But she couldn't go back to sleep. In fact, she couldn't wait to get up. Her mind was racing and, for the first time in weeks, in a positive, not a negative, way. And she felt good, so very good. All the ideas and hopes and shared stories of the last two days had taken hold of her in a powerful, uplifting way that surprised her. She not only was experiencing a change in her perception of her situation, but after last night's goal setting, she was also developing a plan of action that was real—not contrived like some of the other plans she'd learned about.

In the past, when she had heard concepts and methods she didn't like while attending a training session, she would gloss over those parts—like cold calling or handling objections or asking closing questions. She wasn't doing that this time. And that's because she saw none of those chores (especially cold calling—oh, how she hated cold calling) in this concept—none at all.

So she showered and put on one of her best outfits because she wanted to look as good as she felt this morning. Within minutes, she was strolling down Main Street, overlooking the ocean. The morning fog had not burned off yet. There was a newness to this time of the day that she liked. And this morning the day felt newer still, newer than ever before. And she knew why. She checked her satchel again to make sure she had her notebook because she was actually looking forward to reviewing the goals she had written last night with Highground's help.

By the time she got to the coffee shop, Highground was already there looking over the display case of tempting pastries.

"Good morning, Susie!" he chimed, as buoyant as she felt herself. "Ready to start?"

"I've never been more ready in my life."

"Great. Let's get one of these pastries, order up our coffee, grab a table, and review your thoughts from yesterday. Then I'll tell you what you'll experience today."

Within a few minutes, the two were seated at a front table, coffee cups and pastries and notebooks strewn between them. And as Highground looked over Susie's completed goals, his smile grew bigger and bigger and bigger.

"What?" Susie had to know.

"I just love seeing someone like you getting it."

Susie picked up her cup and leaned back confidently in her chair. "You mean, understanding the lifetime value of a relationship—the value of what that person might purchase in a lifetime as well as the value of his or her lifetime referrals? The value of the right communication using a properly organized database that's been ABC-ed? The value of an eight-week goal?"

Highground laid back his head and laughed loud and heartily. "You're doing fabulous, Susie. You're already applying the system to your own style. I'm truly looking forward to seeing the bright future peeking out from the goals you've set for the next eight weeks."

"I appreciate that, Mr. Highground," said Susie, "but I have to admit something. I may be a little uncomfortable telling people that I work this way when I don't—yet. That's the next step, isn't it? I have to start from scratch?"

Highground nodded. "Great observation. Everyone I help through this process has the same hurdle. What you will learn this morning from Philip is how to educate any staff or people that will work with you, then how to educate your clients in your database—your 250 by 250 list that's been ABC-ed. But first, you have to teach yourself. You have to live the system in order to have the confidence to share it with others. That's what being genuine is all about."

"That's a relief. The last thing I want to do is be something that I'm not," she said. "Been there, done that. Doesn't work."

"Do you know how many people never learn that? You're already halfway there."

Highground pushed away from the table when he saw Philip come in the door. "Remember, Susie, Philip is a business-relational, so his style will be quite different from Sheila Marie's or Paul's."

Philip walked in at the appointed time, impeccably dressed as usual. "Good morning, I'm Philip Stackhouse," he said to Susie with a warm, confident smile as he approached the table.

"Philip," Highground said, "this is the friend I was talking about, Susie McCumber."

"Hello, Philip," Susie answered, "it's my pleasure to meet you."

Highground waved him to pull up another chair. "Philip, I was just mentioning to Susie what you will be sharing with her this morning in regards to educating everyone on the system."

"More like indoctrination," Philip laughed, sitting down.

"Before you do, why don't you share with Susie your background and where you were before we met. I thought I would leave you two to talk for a couple of hours before your clients arrive. You are meeting them here, Philip?"

"Yes, I am."

"Well, then, I'll be back about 11:00, okay?"

"No problem," Philip said, and Susie nodded, waving to Highground as he did his disappearing act once more.

"So, Susie," Philip began, leaning toward her. "What do you think of all that you've heard and seen in the last day or so?" Philip had focused suddenly and directly on Susie, almost as if he were interrogating her.

A bit taken aback by this scrutiny, Susie reverted a little into her old nervousness. The fact that Philip was obviously a highly successful individual, based on the way he dressed and acted, didn't help. However, she thought about what she had learned the day before and the fact that she was referred by Highground with nothing to prove to this man. She looked directly at Philip and said, "I still have some questions, but what I like most is I don't have to try to impress you. I just need to be myself. That's what I saw in Sheila Marie and Paul yesterday. Also, the system seemed at first to be a bit simplistic, but I think that's only my first impression. Actually, it's beginning to sound more professional and consistent—if I follow it properly—than any plan I've ever tried, and I don't think that's just wishful thinking."

Susie had forgotten her uneasiness and was on quite a roll, one that Philip noticed. He smiled, impressed. "I think you're going to institute this system as well as anyone I know and I look forward to watching that happen. You are going to truly enjoy the results. So now that you understand and know the value of a relationship, have learned how to create a database and to ABC it, I'm supposed to talk to you about what you do next."

"And what's that?"

"Live it," Philip said, with a wry look. "What do you think of that?"

"Makes sense. How did you achieve that?" Susie asked.

"One step at a time," Philip said. "Understanding how to live this system and educate others doesn't happen overnight. It begins with a perception change—first of yourself, then of others' perception of you. And when that happens, all the people you meet in the future will acquire the new perception immediately."

He waved to get Chuck's attention.

"The usual?" Chuck called over.

Philip shot him his trademark thumbs-up and went back to his conversation. "You know, I hadn't thought of it, but that's what Highground is. He's a perception changer. The first thing he does is change our perceptions of ourselves, which in turn helps us change the perception of those around us."

"He has definitely done that for me in the last two days."

"I wasn't always doing business through my database and by referral," Philip confided. "Before I met Highground I trained the financial planners in my office how to find business cold. I advertised in newspapers, on television, wherever I could spend money in the hope of making the telephone ring. I was pretty good at it. As I moved up the ladder, I always had a knack for selling. I did the wall-to-wall days on the phones as a young securities salesman. I didn't get much fulfillment out of it, but I thought that was how everyone did business."

"You were good at cold calls?"

"I was," Philip admitted. "I just didn't like it. Then I started my own operation and tried to train new sales-people in the art of selling those old ways, and my results plummeted. What I found was there are very few of us out there who learned the techniques to handle objections, isolate the issues, offer solutions, 'close hard three times,' et cetera, to the point of making them work. Rare is the person who is truly good at it or can keep it up over a long time. The more my overall closing percentages went down—because I included my staff in the averages—the more I threw money at places to find more leads. By the time I met Highground, I was at my wit's end. He would say I was on the mantel. I was certainly at a crossroads in my career, very frustrated and disheartened. I was ready to go back to the drawing board and work the phones for ten hours a day. I didn't want to do that, but I knew I could at least pay the bills."

"I know the feeling," Susie said.

"But with a little journey like you are now on, I redirected my business and life. I'm now respected, doing business with who I want to, and have more time to do the things I want to do. My whole staff is trained in this system and they like themselves and the company a lot more for it. When we use the little phrase 'Just let me know,' we understand it is a two-way street. That's why we're so confident when we use it, because we live it."

Susie look at him, puzzled. "Just let me know?"

"Oh, yes. That's the linchpin in Principle 3—Just Let Me Know. Educating your clients about how you work, your value to them, through regular, tangible actions performed without fail. It's what we who have taken Highground's system to heart say to every client we work with. We want them to let us know if we can help them in any way in business or beyond. You'll hear specifically how to make it work with Principle 4. But for now, just know that this phrase is amazing in its power to give the right impression to your clients. The last thing you want to seem is self-serving. Consistently calling and educating your clients about how you work is the most important dynamic in a referral system."

Susie was beaming at this new idea. "I like it. It sounds genuine."

"That's because it is," he explained. "That's the beauty of this program. *It's real.* We help people all the time; we go out of our way to serve our clients in ways that the usual business philosophy would never include. The old-style businessman would not approve—nor would I have only a few years ago. But now it's all part of our service to our clients. When we live that out, the second part of using that phrase becomes second nature."

"What second part? You mean the referral?"

"That's right. Because we are actually living out the principles we tout, we now have a 'hall pass' to ask everyone we know for a referral, and I do mean everyone."

To show her, Philip suddenly took on a warm yet businesslike gaze, sat up professionally straight, looked into her eyes, and said, "So, Ms. Very Important Client, just let me know if we can help you in any way, business or beyond. And if you have any friends or associates that can use our services, please call me with their names. I'll treat them just as I have treated you. Just let us know." He sat back in his chair and smiled. "See?"

Susie grinned. "Yes, I see. That second part is the pivotal part."

Philip nodded. "But it is give-and-take, and people respond to that approach. They really do. And so will you."

Susie suddenly had a thought that made her uneasy. "Do you pay referral fees if someone sends you a client?"

Philip smiled at that. "Good question. One thing I learned from Highground is that we may pay a finder's fee to someone in business if doing so is standard, but as a rule of thumb we normally do not pay a referral fee. You would never expect to be paid to refer a friend to a good restaurant or recommend a movie. You do it because you have received great service or enjoyed the movie, and you think your friend could benefit from knowing about it. You might be appreciated if you go to the restaurant and the owner recognizes you because you are an advocate, and that might get you faster service," he added loud enough to be heard by Chuck, who was coming their way, "much like Chuck here at the coffee shop!"

"Hey, you talking about me?" Chuck said, in a mock-tough voice, setting down a steaming mug of coffee on the table, inches from Philip's lap.

"Hey, it's about time," Philip countered in an even tougher voice. "Here, take the money and leave us alone!"

Chuck laughed, grabbed the money, and then shot him a thumbs-up to Philip's laughing delight.

"That guy is a good man. He's the reason I met Highground. And he's a walking billboard for the success of Highground's system, isn't he?"

"Chuck is involved with this system?" Susie's eyes widened in surprise.

"Sure," Philip said, stirring his coffee and then taking a sip. "Look around at the attention to detail, the group of walking, talking power advocates he has developed."

"He does have a lot of friends and repeat business. You're right."

"And think about the café's 'items of value' you have received in the mail—coupons, discounts for other services, that sort of thing."

Susie couldn't believe she hadn't seen it before. "You're exactly right, Philip. I just realized everything—the language he uses is exactly like the language all of you are teaching me to use. He's always asking me if he can help me in any way. And to pass his name along to any friends or family that would enjoy a good coffee café. He even referred Mr. Highground to me! I just thought . . . well, I don't know what I thought. It was so natural and helpful. Like he cared. And this café is so wonderfully run and its ambiance is so good, why wouldn't I tell my friends about it?"

"That's how it works, Susie. We just pass along the 'good' to those that we like and want to do business with. All of us—Chuck, Paul, Sheila Marie, and many more—we have a whole network of businesses that we are happy to refer to our clients and friends because we know that they are going to take care of them. See how it works?"

"I'm beginning to see the whole, interesting picture."

"Which gets us back to what I'm supposed to talk to you about today—education. Now that you have changed your perception, you need to take the next step and institute some of the 'branding' of the system on your business communications, concepts like 'Just Let Me Know,' along with a host of other pieces that describe your new philosophy: thank-you cards, letterheads, items of value you give to express appreciation. The system needs to be part of what you say to everyone, and you have to demonstrate it daily in your business."

Susie stared at Philip's suit jacket, at something she had been noticing ever since he sat down. "What's the 'Highground' pin on your lapel all about?" she asked. "I've been wanting to ask that since I met you. And I have a feeling that's the point."

"Susie, you are getting it so well!" Philip smiled, tapping his colorful lapel pin. "Do you like it? Several years ago a few of the people who David Michael Highground had helped over the years got together and finally named his wonderful system. We call it 'Highground's Principles of Business.' Highground said it wasn't necessary, but we wanted to do something to honor the man. He is so giving. He really doesn't ask for anything, if you'll notice. He hasn't asked anything of you, has he?"

"No, he hasn't," Susie realized.

"Well, I had to give something back to him. But it also helps me and all of us who live our business and personal lives around this wonderful system. I've incorporated a logo around this name and I include it unobtrusively in certain parts of my literature, explaining the value I put on a lifetime relationship. Everyone is different, so what you use to get this point across is up to you. Okay, you'd better open that notebook of yours. I'm about to give you some great information on Principle 3."

She whipped it and her pencil out, flipped quickly to the right page, and waited. "I'm ready."

"Okay. Principle 3 is—"

Susie interrupted to quote, "Just Let Me Know. Educate your clients about how you work and your value to them through regular, tangible actions performed without fail."

Principle 3: Just Let Me Know. Educate your clients about how you work and your value to them through regular, tangible actions performed without fail.

"Exactly," Philip said, and then in a very no-nonsense tone he began to get down to business. "In a nutshell, it is simply the ability to communicate with everyone you know about how your business works, what you will do for them, and what you expect of them in return. With your ABC-ed database in order, ready and waiting, you're already halfway there. The next step is to educate yourself. When you've changed your perception of yourself and have truly begun to incorporate the language that Highground teaches you into your everyday life, you can move forward." He paused for a second. "Earlier I mentioned the term 'hall pass.' Do you remember in school how you needed a hall pass to have permission to be officially in the halls during class?"

Susie nodded and smiled.

"This is similar in that it is necessary to feel like you have the right to call someone and ask for business. Most of us never communicate with anyone consistently, let alone perform tangible actions demonstrating that the relationship between us and our clients is our first priority. Far too often, I am unable to persuade salespeople to call current and past clients as well as others in their sphere of influence. Why won't they try it? The bottom-line reason—which few of them will admit—is that they are embarrassed for not keeping in touch and feel uneasy and uncomfortable when asked to call now. They've lost their 'hall pass.' What happens, though, when a good keeping-in-touch system is in place? Your calls are welcomed, which is the way people thank you for the professional personal touch in your communications. You have a hall pass to call people and talk business—and feel good about doing it."

Susie wrote furiously, brow furrowed, fully focused, as Philip concentrated on the next point. "Next, if you will have staff working with you, then you have to get them on board. They need to have regular training and live the system well. Once those who will be working with you are on board and are living it, you are now ready to start educating your database list."

Susie looked up. "My 250 by 250 list? The list that I've ABC-ed?"

"That's the one. That's your database list. And you don't have to wait until everything is in place before you start. You just have to start one step at a time.

"The first thing you will send to your ABC database list is *a letter telling everyone of your new business philosophy.* Some refer to this as a confession letter. It simply states the value you place on those you know and/or have served in the past and the new attention you are giving to them. Here's a sample letter I brought for you":

Robert and Carole Rusch
119 Heath Terrace
Rancho Benicia, CA 92117

Dear Bob and Carole:

Recently my staff and I have taken the time to review our business and have come to the unanimous conclusion that the most important assets we possess are the relationships we have developed to date—just like the one we have developed with you.

I also confess that we have not been as proactive in our personal communications as we would have liked. It's to that point that I want you to know we have taken appropriate steps to start communicating more frequently. Be it a newsletter, personal card, or follow-up telephone call from our office, please consider it the tangible evidence that we are putting our relationship with you first in our business.

In the near future, we will be communicating with you personally. Meanwhile, if you have any questions or we can help you in any way, please don't hesitate to call us!

Sincerely,

Philip Stackhouse

Susie handled the letter as if it were a piece of gold. "Sheila Marie mentioned this," she said. "It's perfect." For a few seconds, she studied it hard, her mind spinning with possibilities until a new thought occurred to her—a rather important thought: "What about new people I might meet?"

"The concept still works, and I'll tell you why," he said. "It will become so natural to share how you conduct your business, your relationship system, and its value to others that meeting new people will become a joy. And later, when you follow up with those you meet—first with a personal note immediately after your encounter, of course, and then through your communication program—these people will never feel like they have an L for 'lead' on their foreheads. And you will not have an L for 'loser' on yours because you are making them feel that way!"

Susie laughed. "Well, I'm glad to hear that."

"Consistency is the key, and the people on your database list will—just like your family—know if you are real or not. As they see you 'walk your talk' consistently, they will become believers. Susie, your phone will start to ring regularly with referrals of clients from your database because you have a focused marketing plan that educates them to do it."

One point still bothered Susie. She decided to be honest about it: "How do you handle people who tell you no, Philip? I hate to say it, but I'm still worried about rejection."

Philip smiled. "I'll tell you how to handle that. As soon as you put this proactive 'outbound' philosophy and system in place, you have a way to work around that fear of rejection. You're able to accept that no gracefully and even, possibly, turn it into a yes later if you so choose, with your dignity intact. Tell you what—let's role-play," Philip suggested. "Let's say you're my contact. Assuming I have had permission to communicate with you and have done so regularly, I could feel good about calling you and saying something like this." He pantomimed picking up a phone.

Susie wondered if she should be taking notes. She grabbed her pencil.

Philip began talking into his imaginary phone. "Hello, Susie. This is Philip Stackhouse. Did I catch you at a bad time?'" Philip placed a hand over his invisible phone and stage-whispered to Susie, "Normally, you wouldn't admit to its being a bad time unless you truly were busy."

Playing along, Susie replied, using her pencil as her imaginary phone receiver: "No, no, I'm not busy."

"Great. Susie, *if it's all right with you, I'd like to run a few things by you* concerning the financial gains I've achieved for others in the community in spite of the latest tax law changes. If you like what you hear, we'll take it a bit further. If you don't, we'll leave it at that. Would that be okay?"

Philip put down his imaginary phone. "Now, normally, if I've communicated with you regularly, focused on your needs instead of my own, wouldn't you agree that the chances of your saying yes to talking with me are pretty high?"

Susie nodded her head. "Definitely."

"And you'd be right. Well, then, let's say, for whatever reason, you say no to my request. Now what?" He paused. "This is the big difference—I have a system where most do not. And because I've treated you well, keeping our relationship alive by keeping in touch, if you say no to me, then I am able to respond appropriately. I don't have to overwhelm you or the respectful-yet-professional relationship we have developed. So if you said no to me, this would be my response."

Philip picked up his imaginary phone again and talked into it. "No, Susie? Well, that's fine. I understand. The relationships I develop in this community are certainly more important than selling my products. I'm really enthusiastic over the results I achieve for those I serve, but you certainly need to be the judge of whether this is the right time for you to consider taking advantage of it or not. Perhaps some other time might work better. If it's all right, let's continue to keep in touch. I'll check back with you in another six months. Would that be okay?"

Susie nodded, speaking into her pencil "phone" again. "Yes, that would be fine, Philip. Thank you, anyway. I'll see you."

"See?" Philip said. "Because I have a system in place that follows up with communications that are relational in nature—professional, but still relational—I can easily 'disengage,' keep my dignity in place, and maintain the relationship, if I so choose. I can evaluate it all later."

"Wow!" Susie exclaimed. "If I could say that as smoothly as you just did, my business would take off!"

"You will, because you will have a system behind you. And you will be living out the principles of this system, *evoking the golden rule*. You will actually be treating others as you would want to be treated yourself." Philip paused for emphasis. "Just remember this. When you put this program in place, you must have confidence that it works—as long as you work it."

Susie frowned. "What do you mean?"

"The bottom line is that you must take advantage of your newfound 'hall pass' abilities to call people. You must be proactive and you must ask for the business. Because you are putting the relationship first—keeping in touch regularly, without fail—you will gain new self-esteem and confidence to ask for business and referrals. Your clients will expect it."

Philip finished and sat back, relaxed. Susie, though, was feverishly taking notes.

"The specifics about how to do the rest is Principle 4, which I bet you're going to be learning this afternoon."

"That's right. With someone named Sara Simpson."

"Sara is a dynamo. Get ready to be bowled over. She'll have you learning about the Keep in Touch program within minutes."

"Keep in Touch—"

"That's right," Philip said. "But I'll let her tell you. You'll love it."

Susie finally put down her pencil.

Just then Highground walked in, and they both looked up, amazed that two hours had already passed.

"How is my star student?" he asked.

"She is going to be phenomenal," Philip said, getting to his feet.

"Are you going somewhere?" Susie asked Philip.

"Not far," he said, pointing to the table next to them.

Confused, Susie glanced at Highground.

He explained. "Susie, I'm going to take this seat here with you again. Philip, on the other hand, has a couple coming to meet him here in a few minutes. And he will sit down with them right next to us. That way, we can hear how he educates a new client without making the couple uncomfortable."

"Great idea. I like watching a master in action."

That made Philip grin. "This is a couple I've just started to work with, and I've asked them to come have a cup of coffee with me, to run a few things by them. So this will really help you." That's when he saw the couple come in, right on time. And he went to meet them.

For the next hour, Susie listened intently, amazed as Philip articulated all that he had shared with her that morning. She wished she'd brought a tape recorder.

For several minutes, as Philip and the couple ordered coffee and waited for it to arrive, they talked about the financial planning work he'd done for them. Then, to Susie's surprise and delight, they asked what the Highground pin he was wearing meant. Now Philip had the perfect opening. He stated the philosophy of how he valued a lifetime relationship. And then he presented to them a directory that was titled "In Touch with Friends and Associates." It had his company logo on it. Susie leaned too far over, trying to see the directory, which made the couple look at her. Quickly, she coughed and moved her chair around loudly, working hard to be invisible again, which tickled Highground so much he had to muffle his own laughter. But he couldn't hide his pleasure at her enthusiasm.

"What is this directory?" she whispered to Highground. "That's a great idea!"

"You can do it, too. In fact, you should. It's all your own favorites—your tried-and-true businesses, dry cleaners, convenience stores, restaurants—the very establishments you tell people about all the time. Philip just got smart and printed up his own to give away. He started with a simple list of names on his letterhead. Now he actually produces a little booklet. Listen to how he explains it."

"This is an in-depth listing of all the businesses and services that I can personally recommend in the community," Philip was saying.

THE REFERRAL OF A LIFETIME

Susie wondered if Chuck's California Coffee Café and Bistro and Sheila Marie Deveroux Realty and Paul's auto dealership were all in there. Of course they were, she realized.

And this was the moment that Philip started explaining his philosophy of business, putting the relationship first, living and working by the golden rule. When he stated that he didn't spend any of his time or money in marketing to the general public, that he spent his energies on those he served by bringing them items of value on a regular basis, she quickly started taking a new set of notes.

She wrote as fast as she could, trying to capture his exact speech, especially when he said that if there was any way his staff could be of service, "just let us know."

"You know I mean this," Philip reminded them, since he'd already shown his excellence in the work he'd done for them. "The only thing I ask you is this: if you happen to know of any friends or associates that could use my services, you will think of me. I'll treat them just as I have treated you. This is the way I do business."

Susie gave up. She couldn't write that fast, and this was too good to miss by worrying about getting it all down. She just listened.

And that's when he looked confidently at the couple and said, "You see, the reason you came to me in the first place was because our mutually good friend referred us, remember?"

The couple nodded.

"So I'm dedicated, as you can tell, to upholding the trust that has led us together. Incidentally, *do you know of anyone that might be in need of my services?*"

"I'm sure we do. In fact, our friends the Johnsons could use your help. We just mentioned your name at dinner with them the other evening. We'll make a point of calling them tonight. Just let us write their number down for you."

Susie couldn't believe it. They gave Philip a referral just like he said it would happen! By living and using the system, he had created two power advocates—walking, talking billboards for him and his business.

At this point, Highground motioned to Susie that they needed to leave. Susie and Highground left the coffee shop and started walking down to the dock near where they had eaten lunch the day before.

He stopped by the same bench Susie had sat on to start her 250 by 250 list. *So much had happened since then, it felt like much longer ago,* Susie suddenly thought.

"I believe this spot worked for you yesterday, Susie," Highground was saying. "What I would like you to do is take another twenty minutes or so and write out another step in your goals that you started yesterday—Goal 3. Remember how to do this? Here's a new tape to listen to. Project yourself eight weeks into the future this time. I'll bring you a salad and let you enjoy the quiet for a bit."

The morning fog had given way to a lovely noon sun that set off the brilliant blue ocean, the sight that always confirmed why she had moved here in the first place. She sat down, pulled out her notebook, turned to the third goals page, and began to write:

GOAL 3

Goal: *Professionally brand this system with my own style, then begin a proactive program to use in all that I say and do with all those I know.*

Goal Date: *eight weeks from today.*

The date is *August 15* **and I have:** *everything available for this system in place. From the communication on my business cards, stationery, and fax forms to additional handouts that match up with me and my new philosophy. Because I have worked hard to incorporate this system with my style, I now feel comfortable telling people that I work mainly by referral. I have actual, tangible proof in action all around me. I am educating everyone on a daily basis how I can help them and how they can help me. It is truly a win-win scenario.*

I have already experienced: *ongoing positive response from my clients and all that I come into contact with. I am amazed at the people, many of whom I once thought to have real control of their businesses, wanting to know how I have set all of this up.*

I feel: *more of who I really am. For the first time in my life, I feel genuine about myself because I now have the freedom, or license, to be me. I love my products and what they do for others, and I feel I can competently share them with others in a way that can work for them.*

I am excited about: *helping others take advantage of the benefits my products offer and building and enjoying new relationships. I really am excited about giving them the newfound freedom that Highground has shown me.*

My associates and colleagues are: *impressed with my professional branding of my new system. Many have asked me to tell the people they work with about my experience and how I have achieved it.*

I am determined to: *surround myself with the right visual confirmations that I practice what I preach so I will be genuine in making this system really mine.*

The time flew. Before she knew it, Highground was tapping her on the shoulder, then sitting down beside her to read her new goal. When he finished, he said nothing, gave her a proud smile, and then got up and beckoned her to follow him.

Hurriedly pushing her notebook back into her satchel, she stood up and did just that.

"Ready for Principle 4?" Highground asked, already knowing Susie's answer.

CHAPTER 6

A System That
Works for You

Highground and Susie left the oceanfront and walked up a few blocks from the dock toward Rancho Benicia's downtown area.

As they walked, Highground said, "Well, Susie, you're in the homestretch. Your insights and goals you just wrote prove that you are an amazingly quick study. Before we take this next step to learn the last principle, what specific insights do you have? Anything you want to talk about?"

Susie hesitated, not quite sure she wanted to share her deepest fear with him. He'd now become a sort of mentor to her, and she didn't want to disappoint him. But he had asked, so she told him.

"Mr. Highground, you obviously have helped a number of people through this process. And all you say seems logical. But I guess my biggest hurdle or anxiety is how quickly will I see results? I guess I'm a bit afraid of failure again. I know it should work, but will it really work for me?"

"I appreciate your candor, Susie. You have to be honest with me and with yourself. But believe me—it will work, as long as you trust the process. That is why the first three questions I asked you when we first met were so important. Remember them?"

She nodded. "Do I like myself, do I believe in my products, and can I stay the course?"

"That's right. You are comfortable enough with yourself, you definitely believe in your company's products, and I believe after this next meeting it will all come together for you—how to 'stay the course,' to 'trust the system.' So," he said, stopping for a moment, "are you ready to meet the dynamic Sara Simpson, president of Simpson Systems?"

Susie looked behind her and saw a large, renovated warehouse with a sign hung over its big, artistic, metal doors announcing "Simpson Systems." Susie's eyebrows rose at the very expensive look of it all. But then she nodded.

Highground opened the doors for her. "Remember, Sara is business-business. She is very high-principled or she couldn't run our system so successfully, but she is the daughter of one of the area's first big-business owners and she wants to be known for being her father's daughter— and then some. She proves, though, that this system works for all people once they realize the kind of person they are and are happy to embrace it. Okay, here we go."

They entered the elegantly appointed waiting area. A globe of the world smartly blended into the Simpson Systems logo hanging from the high ceiling. Highground didn't slow, though. He walked straight to the elevator, guiding Susie along with him, stepped inside, and pressed the top floor's button.

In a moment, the doors swooshed open to the executive floor. They approached the two secretaries, who seemed to know Highground by sight, and without a word were escorted into the private conference room of the corner office with the best view of the harbor at Rancho Benicia, overlooking the Baha Mier Cliffs.

This was the war room of Sara Simpson. Highground and Susie had not been there a minute when Sara strode into the room—her high heels clicking and her expensively tailored suit swaying like silk with her every move. She exuded the confidence of a Fortune 500 executive and grinned widely as soon as she laid eyes on Highground.

"David Michael Highground, where have you been? You disappear then reappear at the strangest times. I was just asking Chuck about you. This must be Susan McCumber, the lady you have spoken so highly of. How do you do, Susan?" She stretched out her hand.

For a moment, Susie thought she just might use the more formal and sophisticated "Susan" with this very successful contemporary of hers. But then she remembered that she liked herself just fine. She took Sara's hand and shook it solidly. "My pleasure. And please call me Susie."

Then Sara, all business and proud of it, was off and running. She marched them over to the end of the polished oval table, waved them a command to sit, and began to talk, her total focus on Susie.

"Susie, David has given me an extensive background on you. And what I would like to do for you in the next two and a half hours is give you an in-depth look at our Keep in Touch program—how it works for us, its results, and how it can work for you. Before I do, I would like to give you an idea of where I was before I instituted this program."

The agenda was set and Susie now understood exactly what a business-business person was like.

"Sounds like an excellent plan, Sara," Susie said, with all her businesslike enthusiasm. She was suddenly very interested in how someone who obviously was so business driven actually develops relationships. And it looked as if she might just find out.

"I took over this business at twenty-three," Sara was saying in her clipped speech, as she leaned back in her black leather chair, "when my father died. I was driven for a number of reasons—the loss I felt, the desire to succeed, the need to help out my mother—but mostly I just wanted to prove to the world that Sam Simpson's daughter was able to make it on her own. I did the 'thirty-six-hour' days and gathered all my identity from the business. I became obsessed with it. I drove people in my employ to the brink. I looked at customers as widgets, something that was either a good business decision or not. If they didn't match up with the numbers, they didn't hear from me. My salespeople were the highest paid in the industry, but I drove them until they dropped. Oh, my volume continued to soar and I received all the industry accolades, which invigorated me more. Although my volume increased, the margins were tight because that's the type of clients I ended up with—the shoppers. There was no loyalty."

She glanced at Highground. "I came to a great crossroads in my business five years ago. That's when I met David Highground. I was referred to him by my father's best friend, Paul Fuzak. He had come all the way from New York to visit my family and see me. My dad's friend knew him from childhood and loved him like a brother. What he really was doing out here was checking up on me because he was close to Dad and I reminded him so much of Dad. He really gave me some great insights into who my dad really was—from a business and personal point of view."

She paused, crossing her legs and running a hand along her skirt to straighten it. "You see, I found out why so many people helped me when I started. It was because of my dad's good name.

"Although he was tough as any successful person in business, when it came to helping people through a crisis, especially others in business, he would drop everything he was doing and make himself available. Highground had helped Dad a long time ago when I was young and my dad's friend thought I should meet him. And my life changed dramatically, as well as my business—which was my life, of course. So when he called and asked if I could spend a few hours with you, I couldn't wait for the opportunity—the opportunity to pass it along."

"I really appreciate the insight into your background, Sara," Susie said, meaning it. "Thanks for sharing it."

Sara sat up and leaned across the table. "Well, Susie, let's get down to business. You now understand the lifetime value of a client base; putting the relationship first; the power of 250 by 250; how to build and ABC your database; how to educate your staff, your sphere of influence, your clients and friends; and how to brand all of your communication. In other words, how to live out the golden rule in business. So let's talk about the part of the system that actually delivers on this promise of giving you a 'hall pass' to call everyone you meet, feeling free to talk about helping them while discussing old and new business opportunities. It's Principle 4," Sara went on. "That's 'Keep in touch, consistently, personally, and systemically.'"

Susie scrambled to get her notebook open.

"Good," Sara said, smiling at the notebook. "I remember that notebook. It's your plan of action, your next steps, your lifeline in the beginning. Don't forget that for a minute. Keeping in touch means an ongoing communication that your client base and sphere of influence receive each

Principle 4: Keep in touch, consistently, personally, and systematically.

month consistently, that projects your personal brand. Talking in the language of your ABC-ed list, everyone on your list gets touched in some way, every month. Your As hear from you personally every month. Everyone receives tangible evidence that you do put the relationship first." Sara laughed. "You could be convicted in a court of law for being relational because there is actually some tangible evidence that could be presented as proof—other than our best intentions."

She paused, suddenly thoughtful. "You know, this program is as powerful as any targeted marketing campaign on the street today because it is perpetual and builds a bank account with clients and associates that allows you to go without talking to them for six or seven months. Of course, your Bs and Cs are very impressed because when you do call, they feel like you are talking to them every other week—because you are consistently, personally communicating with them. It's fantastic."

"This morning I heard about 'Just Let Me Know,'" Susie volunteered.

"Wonderful. That is as genuine as it sounds, too. When you actually show consistency with this, you will never feel awkward about saying to anyone 'Just let me know if I can help you in any way. And if you have any friends or associates who could use my services, please give me their names. And I promise to treat them as well as I've treated you.' Of course," she added, "if they haven't heard from you recently or done business with you lately, that might sound self-serving. Your promise will only get the result you want depending how you have treated them. But what you'll find is when you send items along every month that are directed at building the relationship and you have gone out of your way to help them, then you don't come across as self-serving. Your call is always taken. And best of all, people do give you their friends' names. Why? Because they trust you. This program can even knock the edges off a tough businesswoman like me, and because of the professionalism shown in the program, I can demonstrate that I care. And I do, but in my own way."

"That's quite a testimony," Susie said.

"But you know what? In the end, it's not only good for me, but the program was the best decision for the business timewise, too, because I don't have to recreate the wheel every month for new clients. The old ones keep looking for ways to do business with us, and our As are a huge sales force for us because they are our biggest advocates. Having them tell the world—literally—about us is like having a free review written about your restaurant in the *New York*

Times Arts and Leisure section as opposed to taking out a very expensive newspaper advertisement. Make sense?"

"Sure does, but I have a few questions," Susie said as she reviewed her notes from her earlier session with Philip. "What kind of content should I be sending to those in my database?" she asked. "I mean, should I be sending them information about my products or industry? Should I be sending it out in print form or e-mail?"

"Excellent questions, Susie," said Sara. "They are the very ones I struggled with when I began the process. First, when someone asks me if it's smarter to use e-mail or regular mail for a business's communications, I like to respond by saying it's not 'either/or'—it's 'both/and.' We have a CRM system in-house, better known as a customer relationship management system. However, we have added what I refer to as an 'outbound' CRM program in that we are proactive in sending electronic and print communications to those we desire to build relationships with. We refer to it as our Keep in Touch program."

"How do you know which to use when?"

"My rule of thumb is if someone has given us permission to e-mail information to them regarding our business services and can use the information, we send it via e-mail," answered Sara. "But we feel our printed mail tends to make a longer-lasting impression and cannot get deleted as easily as an e-mail. With all the e-mail virus problems, we pick and choose what we send via e-mail and how we send it."

"So you do a lot of printing, then?"

Sara shook her head. "You might be surprised to know that much of our print communications has less to do with our actual business and everything to do with building a relationship. What print material we create is always very professional in style with useful, well-written content—all elegantly designed to make a proper impression. But here is the key. When my sales consultants begin new relationships with new contacts who are currently doing business with the competition or are not ready to do business with us yet, the last thing that works is to flood them with our product information, either in print or e-mail, especially after they have just said they want to think about it. What works is a communication program that simply keeps our names in front of the contact, builds a relationship by giving my people and our brand important 'monthly face time.' This communication program consists of a combination of personal newsletters, holiday cards, and letters containing items of value."

"Items of value?" Susie asked.

"Yes, letters containing unique, simple, useful advice. Everything from free scholarship information for students to how to receive a fiftieth wedding anniversary congratulatory note from the White House. That way, when we follow up for an appointment, our calls are usually taken because they remember our name.

"Of course, if we have a new offering to announce, we include that prospect, but primarily we just want to 'grease the skids' for the next call. Or to use the term you've probably heard by now—to give our people the 'hall pass' to make the call easily. *Business happens on a personal level after a professional impression has been made.* We simply do this in a very systemic way.

"Many corporate suits get hung up on sending information only about their products and industry," Sara went on. "When was the last time you actually read your CPA's newsletter? But you might even refer him if he asked and spent some time and energy relating to you personally. Like I said, business happens on a personal level—after a professional impression is made. You should not be made a slave to the system. It should work even when you don't want to—once you've got it up and going. Is this making sense to you?"

"Absolutely," Susie said. "But it seems more doable for a big operation like yours. How do I do it myself? How does someone like me develop such a program and decide what to send every month?"

Sara thought a moment. "That's a great question. Let me share something with you. When you are a sales organization like ours, you regularly outgrow your infrastructure. That means we often get so busy trying to deliver on our promises that we don't have time to send out everything we should. That's what that old saying means—the one that says every time a business grows by 40 percent, the infrastructure is shot. But here's the new twist for you. It holds true for a company like ours with 300 employees and also yours with one employee.

"So, what's the answer?" Sara said, cocking her head toward Susie. "I bet that's what you're thinking. Well, the answer is that the program needs to be laid out like any good marketing program—one year in advance. Other than special gifts and recognition for your As, you already know the holidays, events, that sort of thing. I recommend that you take the time to focus on getting a basic communication program in place, with the right outsource contractor to handle it, and that you don't come up for air until you have it in place. Got it?"

"Got it . . . I think."

"I'll explain." Sara said. "We split it primarily into two areas: first, our print and e-mail campaign, which we refer to as our Keep in Touch campaign, and second, our Web of Appreciation."

"Web of Appreciation?" Susie looked puzzled.

"Web of Appreciation," Sara repeated. "A very simple system that everyone in our company has access to. It is a series of good, better, and best gifts that we access instantly to show tangible evidence that we care. The program is online, our database is connected, and it takes less than sixty seconds to process. Everyone in our company has a budget of some amount to use to say thank you. We cast our Web of Appreciation as far as we can. The responses are phenomenal. In fact, in our offices we have a wall we refer to as our 'wall of fame' where we post all the responses we receive from our clients and vendors."

"Really! Small tokens of appreciation connect you that well?"

"Let me give you an example," Sara said. "The other day I referred my friend to my chiropractor. When the doctor was finished, he told my friend, 'Thank Sara for the referral.' When my friend told me of the chiropractor's thanks, I was amused at the response. That's the way I used to do it—the way we all did it."

"What was wrong with it?" Susie asked.

"Oh, it was nice to be thanked via my friend. I was happy to help. But for his business's sake, he should have done more—and he could have so easily. What he should have had in place was a simple system whereby he walked past his assistant, told her to thank me for the referral, and sixty seconds later had something tangible such as a gift basket or bouquet of flowers on its way to me. All he needed was my contact information, which he already had, and access to the Internet—which makes it all so easy. And I would have been surprised, impressed, and appreciative of his response. Could he afford something so extravagant? Think about it," she said. "He will probably make more than $1,500 in fees this year from my friend, and he did not have to spend a dime to advertise to find her or convince her that he was the best chiropractor in town because I had already convinced my friend of that fact through the referral. Do you think that gift basket investment makes good business sense? Might even encourage a few more referrals? Certainly does to a true business-business like myself."

Susie responded sheepishly, "I can't say much. I've never done much more than that chiropractor when it comes to showing appreciation. Truth is, I didn't think I had the time or the money to do anything more."

Sara nodded. "Remember, though, as I mentioned, when you can concentrate on setting up your system and have the whole program focused, it very quickly becomes absolutely awesome in its results. It works 24/7 and, like I said, it will work when you don't want to. We process the program and develop certain pieces internally, but we always contract out the new materials and all the Web of Appreciation products. A number of services are available locally, and when they aren't, we can find them on the Internet. As a matter of fact, we outsourced everything for the first three years."

Susie looked at Highground. "You mean, there are companies that will help me set up and deliver these services?"

Highground nodded. "If you want. You can personalize them any way you need to for your own business."

With that, Sara hoisted up two beautifully designed posters with the Simpson Systems logo emblazoned on the front. On the first poster, in big, bold type directly under the company name was the phrase "Keep in Touch." On the second, the bold-type phrase was "Web of Appreciation." The Keep in Touch poster showed a contact suggestion for each of the twelve months of the year. And on the Web of Appreciation poster were the Simpson Systems pledge and its policies, describing how its employees tangibly showed their appreciation to everyone they came in contact with each day. Susie especially took note of the greeting card suggestions.

This is what the two posters looked like:

SIMPSON SYSTEMS
KEEP IN TOUCH

January	— New Year's Greeting Card
February	— Item-of-Value Letter
March	— Personalized Newsletter
April	— Springtime Greeting Card
May	— Item-of-Value Letter
June	— Personalized Newsletter
July	— Fourth of July Card
August	— Item-of-Value Letter
September	— Personalized Newsletter
October	— Item-of-Value Letter
November	— Thanksgiving Card
December	— Personalized Newsletter

SIMPSON SYSTEMS
WEB OF APPRECIATION

We pledge to show tangible evidence of our appreciation for our clients, associates, vendors, and colleagues—regularly, without fail. We put the relationship first!

- All frontline employees are given a budget of $2,000 to utilize as they see fit to say thank you to clients and for customer service relation-stressed situations that require immediate attention.

- The company and its team members recognize all standard gift-giving days throughout the year but pledge to go above and beyond the call of duty to become creative and produce lasting impressions through extraordinary customer service and "outlandish" tasteful items of value.

- Every referral given is recognized immediately, tangibly, and personally the day it is given.

- Every referral that produces business for the company is recognized immediately with more tangible and personal items the day the referral is consummated.

- Extraordinary service by vendors and associates is recognized immediately, tangibly, and personally with appropriate recognition.

- All team members pledge to recognize each other immediately, regularly, and tangibly when character, integrity, and excellence have been demonstrated.

Sara handed Susie letter-size copies of the posters and Susie immediately placed them inside her notebook.

"Our salespeople have a presentation that talks about the lifetime value we place on each client and our program of communication," Sara continued. "Then we follow up with these materials along with our Web of Appreciation, and the results are history. We're number one in our field.

"I don't care what type of business you are in," she added. *"It all boils down to relationships.* Sure, you might re-think some of the items you send, but everything still is connected to your consistency, your follow-through. Remember what I said—business happens at a personal level after a professional impression has been made. With the right system, and motives in the proper order, great things happen."

Susie saw a cross section of all the different types of material sent to the company's ABC database list, which included personalized newsletters featuring articles on personal fitness, success, home, technology, and family and a variety of elegant, personalized greeting cards. All were well planned, all beautifully produced. "But these seem so corporate in design," she had to say.

Sara laughed. "What do you expect from a business-business person like me? You decide, based on your personality, the look and feel of the products that are suitable for you and your type of business and clientele. You have to figure out who you are, be true to that, and plan your designs around that."

"So I can design my own?" Susie wondered.

"If you want to do the Keep in Touch program yourself, you certainly can, but frankly—forgive my directness—it would be foolish to do that. It's much more efficient simply to select the right contractor for you, have your name branded on the products, e-mail or hand off your database, and let the contractor do it so you can concentrate on what you do best. Make sense?"

"Yes, it actually does."

"And," Sara added, "with the simple twelve-month program in place—and it changes every year—you can concentrate on new contacts, moving your Cs to Bs, your Bs to As. You can make all sorts of choices for them—special items of value and appreciation to send them for a referral or help in your business, something to commemorate their special events, and so on. The program should handle all of that. The results of something consistently showing up at your client's door, and the thought that every new contact you have gets included in this concept, is so satisfying that everyone you now meet is in play for your business. When I look at our reports on business coming out of our database, it's absolutely mind-blowing! The average increase in business per client because of the trust built into the relationship—and the minuscule cost of finding a new client because of the resulting referrals, as opposed to what we used to spend on marketing—is incredible." She sat back in her chair and held up her hands in amazement.

"Sounds like you're happy," Susie said, smiling at her enthusiasm.

"Let me put it this way. We used to employ a spray and pray marketing strategy using every advertising and marketing method possible. Now we use a very focused approach to build and maintain relationships for excellent bottom-line results."

"Spoken like a true business-business!" Highground chimed in with a laugh.

"It sounds like a heavy expense," Susie said, still trying to work out in her mind how she would get her program started.

Sara paused. "Susie, let me be direct. There are investments in business and there are expenses. Do you think if my chiropractor invested in a system like this he would generate a few more $1,500-a-year clients?"

"Definitely," Susie stated as she finally started to think beyond her old ways.

"You got it!" Highground exclaimed. "Now, let's go introduce Susie to your sales staff and see how this works. What do you say?"

Sara got to her feet and so did Highground and Susie. "As a matter of fact," Sara said, already headed for the door, "we are just beginning a sales and customer service meeting for some new recruits. Our manager is explaining what 'Just Let Me Know' means and how we introduce the Keep in Touch program, so let's go."

When they walked into the training room, everyone noticed them. Sara gave her team a little go-ahead wave as she seated Highground and Susie and sat down beside them.

The manager was just starting. He gave an overview of the company's commitment to its lifetime clients. He ran a video of a successful national airline commercial that showed a company president telling his sales force that they had just lost their largest and oldest account because they quit using the personal touch that had gotten them the clients in the first place. Then it showed him giving out airline tickets to the salespeople with the command that they were going to "retouch" all they had served in person. And when one of the people asked the company president where he was going, he simply said he was going to see an old friend, referring to the account they had lost.

As the commercial ended, the manager stated that this is the situation their competition is in, losing their clients because of the lack of personal touch. Then he said that this is a situation that Simpson Systems would never be in because of programs called "Keep in Touch" and "Web of Appreciation."

"We have a statement that is almost our slogan," the manager explained. It's 'Just Let Me Know.' And that means if we can help our client in any way—any way at all—we are available at all times. The late founder of this company, Sam Simpson, was always available, and Sara Simpson, our current president, is determined to carry on that tradition, not only in words but in action. The next part of that directive is easy, asking clients to refer their friends and associates with the promise that we will treat them as well as they were treated." He paused and leaned over the podium. "Of course, if you don't treat them that well, the statement will backfire." They all shared a laugh.

He went on to reiterate the Keep in Touch program and the Web of Appreciation, show the wall of fame, and explain the employees' budgets allocated solely to say thank you. Everything Susie heard was exactly what Sara had just taught her. By the time they left, Susie had put the finishing touches on the notes she'd been taking all day long.

As they left the meeting, Susie felt a new sense of confidence. She looked directly into Sara's eyes and thanked her for her time.

"Susie," Sara said, shaking her hand, "in the event things change and you consider the computer field, give me a call. Otherwise, if I can help you in any way, just let me know!" And with a broad smile, she turned on her high heels and went back to work.

As Susie and Highground left the building, Susie had no doubt Sara Simpson meant every word.

"Wow," she said.

Highground smiled. "As I said at the beginning, Sara Simpson proves that the system works for anyone who has the heart for it, no matter what their personal style might be."

"That's the truth."

"Well, it's late," Highground said, checking his watch.

"But I'm learning so much!" Susie said, a little unwilling to let her new mentor go so quickly.

"Data dump," Highground agreed. "In fact, you may have learned too much for one day, not to mention two."

"Oh, I don't think so," Susie said with a laugh. "I am revved."

That made Highground laugh out loud. "I can see that! And I love it. But I want you to let everything simmer, to think about this last principle and how it affects all the rest. Go home and fill in your last goal sheet. And then I want you to review everything in your notebook, making notes to yourself on every point, filling up every blank place with simple, achievable goals and with ideas and questions. Then I'll meet you tomorrow morning at 8:00 A.M. sharp and we will look everything over."

"And then what?"

"And then you begin a whole new chapter in your life," Highground said with a twinkle in his eye. He waved and hurried away, in his disappearing way.

Susie stood there a moment, watching where he had vanished, and she could see the waterfront ahead. And beyond that, she could see the water and the horizon. The sun was going down, dusk was falling, but for some reason she felt like something was dawning in her life, something new. And it felt good.

She rushed home, made dinner, and sat down at her table to fill out the last goal sheet:

GOAL 4

Goal: *Have in place the next twelve months of my Keep in Touch and Web of Appreciation programs.*

Goal Date: *twelve weeks from today.*

The date is *September 15* **and I have:** *laid out the next twelve months of my Keep in Touch program. I have selected the twelve communications that best match my style to be delivered each month. The prewritten communications are in place and the items of value are already ordered. I have a small example of each communication in my portfolio to show those interested in my products and services how I work. I am prepared to demonstrate how I will build the relationship and ask for referrals.*

I have already experienced: *so much positive response and business through my system that it's hard to believe the hopelessness I felt only months before because I did not have a plan of action that suited me.*

I feel: *proud of the hard work I have done and the discipline I have shown to execute this program so well. I feel a sense of accomplishment because of its completion as well as the business I have experienced.*

I am excited about: *the prospect of hiring an assistant to help with administering the system while I spend my time helping other people with my products.*

My associates and colleagues are: *blown away by the completeness of the Keep in Touch and Web of Appreciation system I have in place and the success it is producing. I, on the other hand, am happy that I can be genuinely me and not have to try to be something I am not.*

I am determined to: *continue with this program and deliver it consistently so I may concentrate on the things I like to do—serve my clients and help them reach their goals in life, too.*

Susie sat back, laid her pen down, and looked at her last goal. Then she flipped back to the beginning of her notebook to scan the other three goals along with the principles, and her eyes landed on her first hastily jotted attempt at her 250 by 250 list. *Principle 1*, she thought: *The 250 by 250 Rule. It's not only who you know that counts, it's who your clients know that is important.* There were over 160 names on it. She looked them over one by one, getting more excited with each name.

And she began to automatically ABC them all, jotting down the appropriate letter by each name, checking the ones she'd tried the first day for practice to see if she still agreed with her rankings.

Principle 2, she thought with a smile: *Build a database and ABC it.* Now she could see how the list worked. In fact, she was actually looking forward to having this great reason to reconnect with some of these old, familiar names—after she had sent out her confession letter.

Principle 3: Just Let Me Know. Educate your clients about how you work and your value to them through regular, tangible actions performed without fail, she quoted proudly to herself. *And Principle 4: Keep in touch, consistently, personally, and systematically.*

Interesting, she thought, shaking her head. She realized that she remembered all four principles of the system easily. The best part, though, was that she could see how the whole plan worked, all right here before her. It was truly simple, with amazingly deep, ongoing results—this wonderful system that puts the relationship first because its foundation is based on the simplest of all ideas: the golden rule.

She closed the notebook and rested her hand on it. "Oh my," she mumbled, grinning to herself. "I'm going to have a hard time sleeping tonight."

And she was exactly right.

CHAPTER 7

A Brand New Attitude

The next morning, Susie woke far too early again. She got dressed, grabbed her notebook, and took the long way to Chuck's café, savoring this new feeling and this moment in her life. It still felt like a beginning. And it felt good.

At 8:00 A.M., she walked into the café. And there was Highground chatting with Chuck behind the counter. They both greeted her with big smiles, and Highground strolled over, waving her to a table up front where they could see the water.

"How are you doing this morning?" Highground wanted to know as they sat down.

"Oh, Mr. Highground. Great, just great!"

That pleased Highground tremendously. "I can see the transformation happening before my eyes. You are hardly the same woman I met three days ago."

"Thanks to you."

"No," Highground corrected her. "No matter how much knowledge you gain about the system, it only works if you stay true to the three questions I asked you. And I think you will."

"That's my plan."

"Let's get out your notebook."

Susie zipped out the notebook and plopped it open to the Goal 4 page she had filled in the night before.

Highground examined it and nodded approvingly, patting the notebook. "Susie, what I'd like for us to do this morning is to review all you've experienced the last couple of days and then talk about your plans for the future—your newfound plan of action. Okay?"

Susie sighed. "I have to tell you, Mr. Highground. Philip called you a perception changer, and that is exactly what you are. You change perceptions, which changes attitudes. I have often told people to cheer up or look at the bright side of things, but there's no way to do that when we are dodging falling trees, as you put it. A person's attitude can only change when his or her perception changes, and that's what you, along with your friends, have done for me the past couple of days. For that I am very appreciative."

That seemed to please him deeply. "Thank you. But, as I said, it's really up to you now."

"But now I know the combination!" Susie said, pointing to the notebook page before them. It was the "Right Combination for Success" drawing of Principle 4 that showed all four principles and the lock popped open. "You know, I smiled when I saw that last lock open on Principle 4 the very first day you gave me the notebook, even before I knew about the power of putting a Keep in Touch program in place. Now it makes me smile even more."

Highground cocked his head at the picture and smiled, too. "The combination can unlock a whole new world." Highground flipped back to her goal sheets. "And from the looks of these goals, you're halfway there. You have projected yourself into the future several weeks for each goal and done it admirably. And your tasks are simple and achievable, which makes each goal reasonably attainable. Good for you. My bet is you'll attain them."

That made Susie beam.

"You know where I'd like us to start?" he suddenly decided. "Why don't you explain to me where you were two days ago and where you are right now."

Susie laughed. "Do you realize I almost didn't call you because I was concerned about my cell phone bill? That's where I was. My biggest frustration was that I had no plan for who I talked to about my business or what to do with them after I made contact. I was either coming on too strong or I simply couldn't connect with them at all, so how could I develop a relationship?

"I thought I needed some grandiose marketing or advertising plan that would save me. I was continually looking toward tomorrow and hoping the perfect plan would just appear. When it didn't, I hit the wall and that's when we met. You know," she realized, "strangely enough, what I had been hoping for did appear—when Chuck referred me to you."

That's when Chuck appeared at her elbow carrying her usual hazelnut coffee with steamed milk and a biscotti, just like the one he pushed toward her three days earlier to coax her into telling him her problems. He pushed it—ceremoniously—across the table toward her.

Susie loved the gesture, laughing out loud.

"It's amazing what seventy-two hours can do for a person, isn't it?" Chuck said, patting Highground on the shoulder before going back to his work.

"How long ago did he begin your system?" Susie asked Highground, gazing appreciatively back Chuck's way.

"About five years ago. And it may not surprise you to know that he was referred to me by a friend of his, too."

"No, that doesn't surprise me at all—now." She dunked her biscotti into her coffee and took a big bite out of it.

"So go on. You left off at the point Chuck referred me, I believe."

"Well, you know what happened after that. Now I have a proactive plan that fits me. I don't feel the need to try to imitate someone else," she said.

"And I understand and appreciate the old saying that *it's eleven times more expensive to find a new client than to keep an existing one*," she added, enjoying her biscotti. In fact, she seemed to be enjoying everything more this morning.

"My problem was I didn't have a system in place to keep my existing clients by communicating with them regularly enough, let alone ask them for referrals. But I now have your system, the system that puts the relationship first and is based on the golden rule and that can demonstrate my consistency and earn me the right to ask and receive, hopefully, referrals from my special people."

"As soon as you begin to live it, Susie, it is your system. You will experience the success of staying the course."

"And I'll be proud to claim it because it seems to me that the beauty of this system, especially the Keep in Touch program, is the way it communicates. So many people talk about communicating with their database, but few do, other than an occasional mailer trying to sell something else or brag about themselves. But I truly believe that when I tell my client to just let me know if I can help them, I will be prepared to. And then when I ask if they have any friends or associates that could use my services and promise to treat them as I have treated the client, it will mean something. Because I've proved myself through consistency, right? Through staying the course, by staying in touch."

Highground sat back and shook his head. "That is such a nice way of putting it." He looked proudly at his new student. "It's obvious you have come into your own now, Susie. This is always such a high point for me."

But Susie wasn't finished. "You know, before I met you, if someone gave me a card, I put it in a file and never did follow up appropriately. When I finally got around to calling about something I was offering, so much time had passed since the last time I'd made contact, I felt like a fake, a counterfeit, calling and acting as if I were interested in the relationship. But both of us knew the only reason I was truly calling. I was acting like an opportunist, and the way that made me feel was what was holding me back. My stomach kept turning. I know that now."

Susie smiled. "But everything is going to change. Now, I will be doing things the old-fashioned way—I will earn the right to ask for a referral. I understand these great principles and how they apply to business. I will be in touch with the people in my life on a regular basis, and I now know how to actually do that, communicating with them and consistently offering them items of value. And I have a sneaky feeling that many of them will be impressed for the sole reason that they have always wanted to do this kind of communication themselves but never knew exactly how."

Highground lifted his coffee cup in a toast to Susie. So Susie lifted hers, too. "You should be proud of yourself, Susie. I salute you."

"Thank you," Susie said and clinked her coffee cup with his, then dunked the last of her biscotti and popped it in her mouth. "You can't imagine how proud I am of myself.

But I'll be more proud once this whole system is up and rolling and I'm living it every day."

"Exactly. You have an excellent grasp of the system. Now I encourage you to stay the course for four months. Work at it, Susie. Do it. Because if you do, you will settle into a routine that will be unique to you."

Highground placed a piece of paper on Susie's notebook. "Put this in your notebook. It's what I call my 'Next Steps List.' It is simply a list of the twenty most important next steps, events to schedule into your day to get this process going. Once the system is set, you have an instant relational gateway into every new contact you make, and you have the special ability to touch everyone regularly, without fail. Just set it into motion and stay the course. Remember, after you have demonstrated consistency with clients you already have relationships with, you will never have competition again. You will own the relationship in the same wonderful way that you can claim a friend."

Susie looked excitedly at the Next Steps List and immediately began to make notations on it, thinking ahead to when she could get started on everything.

NEXT STEPS LIST

1. Finish the list of initial names. Call and verify addresses, telephone numbers, and e-mail addresses.

2. ABC all names.

3. Select a contact manager or CRM system. Make sure you have the ability to set ABC fields.

4. Research and select a trusted contract database professional with mail and print service.

5. Research the Internet for different communications you can develop for your Keep in Touch program. Check with those in your industry to see what they use. Outline a twelve-month program.

6. Select an online-service to help you develop and deliver an immediate Web of Appreciation. Make sure you can access your database for ease of use with standard selections that can be processed without difficulty.

7. Purchase personalized thank-you notes. Immediately send them after every meeting upon gaining permission to add the person to your database.

8. Finalize a twelve-month Keep in Touch print program for your database. Select the items and choose the dates when you will send them. Commit the plan to paper and make it visible. List the program tasks needed each month to deliver without fail.

9. Finalize a Web of Appreciation program. Set an appropriate budget for frontline personnel, referral gifts, and standard holiday gifts in addition to your Keep in Touch program.

10. Send a confession letter to your database.

11. Follow up by calling everyone you have sent a letter to. Ask for birthdays (not years) and anniversaries if appropriate. Enter them into your database.

12. Set personal meetings with your As and explain your new philosophy. *Ask for referrals during each meeting.*

13. If needed, make a commitment to a set number of personal appointments or telephone calls to add more potential clients to your database. Utilize the three magic questions.

14. If you want a larger sphere of influence, adopt a database. Call everyone on your newly adopted list and ask permission to start communicating.

15. If you want a larger sphere of influence, select a direct-mail list. Customize the list and call each person using the qualifying question Sheila Marie used to build a relational farm.

16. Educate everyone on your staff about how the program works. Incorporate the principles into your culture.

17. Call all the people who "make money when you make money"—primarily your vendors. Explain how your program works, ask what you can do for them, and then *ask for referrals.*

18. Incorporate into your sales presentation how you put relationships first and what the value is to your clients. Share your new philosophy with everyone appropriate who will listen. Then *ask for referrals.*

19. Use your newfound 'hall pass' and make a scheduled call to everyone in your database at least once a year. If you have developed a birthday card program, make the call after you have sent out the birthday card, calling to say "happy birthday." Ask how you might help the person and ask for a referral or an appointment if appropriate.

20. Always, always ask what you might do for the person you call and always, always remind the person

that your business is built on the good opinion of others. Then always *ask for a referral*—just like Philip did.

When she finished scanning the list, she noticed that Highground had stood up. "You are going to do great, Susie. Make sure you check off each one after you complete it, then list these steps in your planner with your goals and stay true to your promise to me and yourself. Stay the course." He smiled. "It's been a pleasure getting to know you. If I can help you in any way at all, just let me know. And if you have any friends that can benefit from the concepts I shared, pass them on. Share them, and you will be personally blessed by doing so. It's the good stuff—it's the golden rule!"

"Do you have to leave?" Susie said, suddenly rather sad.

"See you, old friend!" she heard Chuck call from behind her. She looked around at Chuck, and when she turned back, the mysterious Mr. Highground had disappeared yet again.

She could only shake her head and smile after him. Chuck walked up and began picking up their dirty dishes. "Quite a guy, huh?"

Susie could only shake her head again. She picked up her notebook and the Next Steps List that Highground had given her, then got to her feet, too. And with a big smile for Chuck, she said, "You know, the day is young and I'm ready to get going. See you later, Chuck."

Chuck watched Susie leave. She had a confidence in her step that was missing a few days ago. "The high ground will do that for you," he murmured, picking up the last of their dishes and feeling a deep sense of satisfaction at his role in the drama. *Susie McCumber's professional transformation,* he thought to himself, enjoying the sound of it. He liked Susie, and he had no doubt the high ground was for her.

Besides, he realized with a happy smile as he headed back behind his antique oak counter, it didn't hurt that even though there were other coffee places in town, there would be only one that Susie McCumber would continue to frequent, not to mention tell all her friends and clients about—and that was the California Coffee Café and Bistro.

The Referral of a Lifetime

It was another perfect morning at the California Coffee Café and Bistro as the regulars, including Susie McCumber, lined up for their morning cups of "the usual" before starting their day.

There was a monumental difference in the Susie Mc-Cumber of today compared to the Susie of six months prior. This Tuesday morning, like every Tuesday morning, Susie had her team of five employees seated out front for their weekly meeting. Her business had exploded, prompting the hiring of two additional salespeople, another customer service person, and a personal assistant. Susie had a relaxed air of confidence about her—not boastful, just confident.

Every month, every person in her company database received an outstanding monthly communication. They were so impressive, Chuck started pinning them up on his bulletin board. She became well known for her flair for business referral thank-yous that were always offered in appropriate yet memorable ways. Susie had quickly discovered she was a business-relational and developed her strengths around that fact. She was truly free to be herself and her business showed the results.

Philip walked into the busy shop, grabbed a copy of the *Wall Street Journal*, and stood in line directly behind Susie. Tapping her on the shoulder, he said, "Good morning." Glancing at the size of Susie's team assembled for her meeting, he smiled. "It appears you got past your concern about people telling you no since your growing team suggests that you have gotten a lot of yeses."

"It's been a great experience, Phil. I'm the same person. I just got comfortable with the gifts I was given and learned to run with them—with a little help from my friends. I found with the momentum I built through the help of the system, I could really get past the tension of having to make a sale. You know what I mean—I could focus on my clients' needs instead of mine. As soon as I started doing that consistently, putting the relationship first, invoking the golden rule daily, business started coming to me. That philosophy removed the dollar signs from my forehead. And you were a great resource, Phil."

The phone behind the antique oak bar rang and Chuck, in the middle of preparing a double cappuccino, no whip, stopped, grabbed it, talked a second, then turned and looked at Susie. "It's for you."

Susie frowned, confused. After all, she hadn't had her coffee yet. "Who is it?"

Chuck handed her the phone and returned to his coffee creation. "A friend of yours."

"Hello?" Susie said tentatively into the receiver.

"Susie! Highground here. How are you? It's been six months."

That woke her up. "I'm just great, Mr. Highground. How are you? I've loved getting your postcards from all over. You've been on the move."

"Just helping out a few friends. I'm back in town now. And I've been hearing good things about you. I just want to thank you for keeping your promise about staying the course. It sounds as if you are doing fabulously, and I'm really happy for you."

"Oh, thank you. It has been fabulous. Absolutely! I can't wait to tell you the whole story."

"Well, I can't wait to hear it. Which brings me to why I called. I do have a favor to ask of you."

"Anything."

"I have a new friend that needs some help and I wanted to know if you could meet us tomorrow and—"

"Talk about one of the principles and share where I was and where I am now? You bet. It would be my utter pleasure. I'll be here."

Susie handed the phone back to Chuck with one hand and took her hazelnut coffee with steamed milk from him with the other.

"Everything okay?" he asked, hanging up the phone.

"Better than okay," she answered with a grateful shake of her head. "And all because of you."

Susie took a few steps away, then stopped, turned back to Chuck, and said, "You know something, Chuck? He really was the referral of a lifetime."

Highground's Principles of Business

This appendix is designed as a reference to help you implement the principles and concepts of *The Referral of a Lifetime*. The appendix contains the following material:

- Highground's Principles of Business
- Highground's Principles of Business Questions
- Letter of Introduction to Past Clients
- Confession Letter
- Highground's Principles Goal Pages
- Three Magic Questions for New Contacts
- The Four Business Personality Windows
- Keep in Touch Suggestions
- Web of Appreciation Pledge and Policies Sample
- Highground's Twenty Next Steps

HIGHGROUND'S PRINCIPLES
OF BUSINESS

These are the four foundational principles of the system. To find out more, return to chapters 3, 4, 5, and 6.

PRINCIPLE 1: The 250 by 250 Rule. It's not only who you know that counts, it's who your clients know that is important.

PRINCIPLE 2: Build a database and ABC it.

PRINCIPLE 3: Just Let Me Know. Educate your clients about how you work and your value to them through regular, tangible actions performed without fail.

PRINCIPLE 4: Keep in touch, consistently, personally, and systematically.

HIGHGROUND'S PRINCIPLES OF BUSINESS QUESTIONS

These reflective questions are the starting point for deploying the system. To find out more, return to chapter 1.

QUESTION 1: Do you like yourself?

QUESTION 2: Do you believe in your product and company?

QUESTION 3: Are you willing to "stay the course"?

LETTER OF INTRODUCTION TO PAST CLIENTS

This letter can be used to assign existing clients to a new sales or customer service person. To find out more, return to chapter 4.

Ken and Sue Turek
1007 Pacific Coast Way
Rancho Benicia, CA 92117

Dear Ken and Sue:

I want you to know how much I appreciate the fact that you chose our dealership to purchase your new BMW from. I, along with the members of our team, want you to know that if you have any questions, any problems, please feel free to call us directly.

It is to that end that I asked our new manager, Paul Kingston, to work with you personally in the event you have any questions or needs. Paul is a proven professional and we are proud to be associated with him. He always puts the relationship first with everyone he serves.

Paul will be contacting you in the near future simply to personally introduce himself and answer any questions you might have.

Thanks again!

Warm regards,

P. J. Stoddart
President
Rancho Benicia AutoGroup, Inc.

CONFESSION LETTER

This letter can be used as the first mailing to those you have neglected to keep in touch with and now want to communicate with regularly. To find out more, return to chapter 5.

Robert and Carole Rusch
119 Heath Terrace
Rancho Benicia, CA 92117

Dear Bob and Carole:

Recently my staff and I have taken the time to review our business and have come to the unanimous conclusion that the most important assets we possess are the relationships we have developed to date—just like the one we have developed with you.

I also confess that we have not been as proactive in our personal communications as we would have liked. It's to that point that I want you to know we have taken appropriate steps to start communicating more frequently. Be it a newsletter, personal card, or follow-up telephone call from our office, please consider it the tangible evidence that we are putting our relationship with you first in our business.

In the near future, we will be communicating with you personally. Meanwhile, if you have any questions or we can help you in any way, please don't hesitate to call us!

Sincerely,

Philip Stackhouse

HIGHGROUND'S PRINCIPLES GOAL PAGES

These goal sheets can be used to plan your personal program. To view completed goals, return to pages 54, 56, 76–77, and 98.

GOAL 1

Goal: *Finish my 250 by 250 list and then organize the names. Begin to put my new mind-set into action.*

Goal Date: _____

The date is _____ and I have:

_____

_____

_____

_____

_____

_____

I have already experienced:

_____

_____

I feel:

_____

_____

I am excited about:

_____

_____

My associates and colleagues are:

_____

_____

I am determined to: _____

_____

_____

GOAL 2

Goal: *Have my 250 by 250 database ABC-ed and in use.*

Goal Date: _____

The date is _____ and I have:

_____

_____

_____

_____

_____

I have already experienced:

_____

_____

I feel:

_____

_____

I am excited about:

_____

_____

My associates and colleagues are:

_____

_____

I am determined to: _____

_____

_____

_____

GOAL 3

Goal: *Professionally brand this system with my own style, then begin a proactive program to use in all that I say and do with all those I know.*

Goal Date: _____

The date is _____ and I have:

_____

_____

_____

_____

_____

I have already experienced:

_____

_____

I feel:

_____

_____

I am excited about:

_____

_____

My associates and colleagues are:

_____

_____

I am determined to: _____

_____

_____

_____

GOAL 4

Goal: *Have in place the next twelve months of my Keep in Touch and Web of Appreciation programs.*

Goal Date: _____

The date is _____ and I have:

_____

_____

_____

_____

_____

_____

I have already experienced:

_____

_____

I feel:

_____

_____

I am excited about:

_____

_____

My associates and colleagues are:

_____

_____

I am determined to: _____

_____

_____

_____

THREE MAGIC QUESTIONS
FOR NEW CONTACTS

These simple questions will help engage you immediately with new people you meet. To find out more, return to chapter 3.

1. What is it you do?

2. What do you like most about that?

3. If you could start over, knowing what you now know, what would your day look like?

Bonus follow-up statement to use whenever you choose: "Tell me more."

THE FOUR BUSINESS
PERSONALITY WINDOWS

The four personality types are expressed in two words. The first word, on the left of the hyphen, represents how people see you and who you are naturally. The word on the right of the hyphen represents your natural tendency in business relationships.

Relational-Relational

Relational-Business

Business-Relational

Business-Business

Relational-Relational

The relational-relational person is one who only thinks of relationships with others—how to help them and how to be liked or even loved. These people rarely think of the business ramifications of their actions, or if they do, they will justify them immediately in some relational way. So the second word has to be "relational," too.

Relational-Business

When meeting people, the relational-business person is truly interested in the relationship, but when the talk turns to business, this person will begin to think strategically.

Business-Relational

The business-relational person doesn't seem at first glance as interested in a relationship as much as in pure business, but this person will develop deep relationships after the business is established.

Business-Business

This trait is simply the opposite of relational-relational. Business-business people normally have a hard time with relational principles and the concepts of this system until they justify in some purely business way the time spent with those they've affected—which they always do.

KEEP IN TOUCH
SUGGESTIONS

January	• New Year's Greeting Card
February	• Item-of-Value Letter
March	• Personalized Newsletter
April	• Springtime Greeting Card
May	• Item-of-Value Letter
June	• Personalized Newsletter
July	• Fourth of July Card
August	• Item-of-Value Letter
September	• Personalized Newsletter
October	• Item-of-Value Letter
November	• Thanksgiving Card
December	• Personalized Newsletter

WEB OF APPRECIATION PLEDGE
AND POLICIES SAMPLE

We pledge to show tangible evidence of our appreciation for our clients, associates, vendors, and colleagues—regularly, without fail. We put the relationship first!

- All frontline employees are given a budget of $2,000 to utilize as they see fit to say thank you to clients and for customer service relation-stressed situations that require immediate attention.

- The company and its team members recognize all standard gift-giving days throughout the year but pledge to go above and beyond the call of duty to become creative and produce lasting impressions through extraordinary customer service and "outlandish" tasteful items of value.

- Every referral given is recognized immediately, tangibly, and personally the day it is given.

- Every referral that produces business for the company is recognized immediately with more tangible and personal items the day the referral is consummated.

- Extraordinary service by vendors and associates is recognized immediately, tangibly, and personally with appropriate recognition.

- All team members pledge to recognize each other immediately, regularly, and tangibly when character, integrity, and excellence have been demonstrated.

HIGHGROUND'S TWENTY NEXT STEPS

This list of next steps can be used as a checklist to implement your personal system.

1. Finish the list of initial names. Call and verify addresses, telephone numbers, and e-mail addresses.

2. ABC all names.

3. Select a contact manager or CRM system. Make sure you have the ability to set ABC fields.

4. Research and select a trusted contract database professional with mail and print service.

5. Research the Internet for different communications you can develop for your Keep in Touch program. Check with those in your industry to see what they use. Outline a twelve-month program.

6. Select an on-line service to help you develop and deliver an immediate Web of Appreciation. Make sure you can access your database for ease of use with standard selections that can be processed without difficulty.

7. Purchase personalized thank-you notes. Immediately send them after every meeting upon gaining permission to add the person to your database.

8. Finalize a twelve-month Keep in Touch print program for your database. Select the items and choose the dates when you will send them. Commit the plan to paper and make it visible. List the program tasks needed each month to deliver without fail.

9. Finalize a Web of Appreciation program. Set an appropriate budget for frontline personnel, referral gifts, and standard holiday gifts in addition to your Keep in Touch program.

10. Send a confession letter to your database.

11. Follow up by calling everyone you have sent a letter to. Ask for birthdays (not years) and anniversaries if appropriate. Enter them into your database.

12. Set personal meetings with your As and explain your new philosophy. *Ask for referrals during the meeting.*

13. If needed, make a commitment to a set number of personal appointments or telephone calls to add more potential clients to your database. Utilize the three magic questions.

14. If you want a larger sphere of influence, adopt a database. Call everyone on your newly adopted list and ask permission to start communicating.

15. If you want a larger sphere of influence, select a direct-mail list. Customize the list and call each person using the qualifying question Sheila Marie used to build a relational farm (see pages 31–32).

16. Educate everyone on your staff about how the program works. Incorporate the principles into your culture.

17. Call all the people who "make money when you make money"—primarily your vendors. Explain how your program works, ask what you can do for them, and then *ask for referrals.*

18. Incorporate into your sales presentation how you put relationships first and what the value is to your clients. Share your new philosophy with everyone appropriate who will listen. Then *ask for referrals.*

19. Use your newfound 'hall pass' and make a scheduled call to everyone in your database at least once a year. If you have developed a birthday card program, make the call after you have sent out the birthday card, calling to say "happy birthday." Ask how you might help the person and ask for a referral or an appointment if appropriate.

20. Always, always ask what you might do for the person you call and always, always remind the person that your business is built on the good opinion of others. Then always *ask for a referral—* just like Philip did.

ABOUT THE AUTHOR

Tim Templeton is an internationally recognized authority in sales processes, systems, presentation, and productivity. He has lectured, trained, and consulted for organizations in multiple industries and countries. His products have been translated into numerous languages.

Tim is a senior partner in Always Positive, a full-service sales and marketing solutions firm. Always Positive specializes in sales training, sales products, and incentives and is dedicated to "making measurable differences" for the companies it serves. He also serves as spokesman and consults and develops content and training for RES, an innovation leader for productivity tools that serves the real estate industry.

In 1991, Tim began his training career, contributing to the book *The Entrepreneurs Handbook* by James C. Ray (Irwin Professional Publishing). In 1995, Tim incorporated and cofounded Providence Seminars and served as CEO.

Throughout the '80s, Tim successfully launched and represented dozens of products both nationally and regionally throughout the retail industry.

Tim serves on the national board for The Center for Faithwalk Leadership, a nonprofit organization cofounded by Ken Blanchard. He is a certified facilitator of Leadership Encounter, a two-day, faith-based workshop for businesses and individuals developed by The Center for Faithwalk Leadership and based on *Leadership by the Book* by Ken Blanchard, Bill Hybels, and Phil Hodges.

Tim resides in the San Diego area with his wife, Maria, and their daughters, Sara, Sheila, and Susie. They are his "delight and the center of his universe."

SERVICES AVAILABLE

Tim Templeton is available for executive consultation or to motivate and train your group or organization. In addition, Always Positive customizes and institutes Keep-INTouch™ programs and the Web of Appreciation™ for its clients as well as develops incentive programs for companies and individuals who desire to incorporate the principles of this book into their business.

For more information contact

Always Positive
Marketing Director
Toll free: 877-321-6500
E-mail: info@alwayspositive.com
Web sites: www.alwayspositive.com
www.realtyempowerment.com
Book comments: comments@alwayspositive.com

Berrett-Koehler Publishers

B errett-Koehler is an independent publisher of books and
other publications at the leading edge of new thinking and
innovative practice on work, business, management, leadership,
stewardship, career development, human resources, entrepre-
neurship, and global sustainability.

Since the company's founding in 1992, we have been committed
to creating a world that works for all by publishing books that
help us to integrate our values with our work and work lives, and
to create more humane and effective organizations.

We have chosen to focus on the areas of work, business, and
organizations, because these are central elements in many
people's lives today. Furthermore, the work world is going
through tumultuous changes, from the decline of job security to
the rise of new structures for organizing people and work. We
believe that change is needed at all levels—individual, organiza-
tional, community, and global—and our publications address each
of these levels.

To find out about our new books,
special offers,
free excerpts,
and much more,
subscribe to our free monthly eNewsletter at

www.bkconnection.com

Please see next pages for other books
from Berrett-Koehler Publishers

Be a Sales Superstar
21 Great Ways to Sell More, Faster, Easier in Tough Markets

Tracy shares the most important principles for sales success he has discovered in 30 years of training more than a half million sales professionals in 23 countries. Concise and action-oriented, *Be a Sales Superstar* is a handbook for busy sales professionals, providing key ideas and techniques that will immediately increase your effectiveness and boost your results.

Hardcover, 128 pages • ISBN 1-57675-175-9
Item #51759-415 $19.95

Goals!
**How to Get Everything You Want
—Faster Than You Ever Thought Possible**

Goals! explains the seven key elements of goal setting and the 12 steps that are necessary to set and accomplish goals of any size. You'll learn to determine your strengths, what you truly value in life, and what you really want to accomplish in the years ahead.

Paperback original, 300 pages • ISBN 1-57675-235-6
Item #52356-415 $24.95

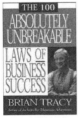

The 100 Absolutely Unbreakable Laws of Business Success

In this eye-opening practical guide, Brian Tracy presents a set of principles or "universal laws" that lie behind the success of business people everywhere. It will teach you how to attract and keep better people, produce and sell more and better products and services, control costs more intelligently, expand and grow more predictably, increase your profits, and much more.

Paperback, 336 pages • ISBN 1-57675-126-0
Item # 51260-415 $14.95

Hardcover, 300 pages • ISBN 1-57675-107-4
Item #51074-415 $24.95

Also available on audiocassette

Berrett-Koehler Publishers
PO Box 565, Williston, VT 05495-9900
Call toll-free! **800-929-2929** 7 am-9 pm Eastern Standard Time
Or fax your order to 802-864-7627
For fastest service order online: **www.bkconnection.com**

Berrett-Koehler books and audios
are available at quantity discounts
for orders of 10 or more copies.

The Referral of a Lifetime

The Networking System That Produces Bottom-Line Results... Every Day!

Tim Templeton

Hardcover
144 pages
ISBN 1-57675-240-2
Item #52402-415 $19.95

To find out about discounts on orders of 10 or more copies for individuals, corporations, institutions, and organizations, please call us toll-free at (800) 929-2929.

To find out about our discount programs for resellers, please contact our Special Sales department at (415) 288-0260; Fax: (415) 362-2512. Or email us at bkpub@bkpub.com.

Subscribe to our free e-newsletter!

To find out about what's happening at Berrett-Koehler and to receive announcements of our new books, special offers, free excerpts, and much more, subscribe to our free monthly e-newsletter at www.bkconnection.com.

Berrett-Koehler Publishers
PO Box 565, Williston, VT 05495-9900
Call toll-free! **800-929-2929** 7 am-9 pm Eastern Standard Time
Or fax your order to 802-864-7627
For fastest service order online: **www.bkconnection.com**